The Wit and Wisdom
of Quentin Crisp

*Also from Alyson Books
by Quentin Crisp*

RESIDENT ALIEN

HOW TO HAVE A LIFE-STYLE

The Wit and Wisdom of Quentin Crisp

Compiled and edited by
Guy Kettelhack

alyson
books

LOS ANGELES • NEW YORK

Manufactured in the United States of America.
Printed on acid-free paper.

This trade paperback is published by Alyson Publications Inc.,
P.O. Box 4371, Los Angeles, California 90078-4371.
Distribution in the United Kingdom by Turnaround Publisher Services Ltd.,
Unit 3 Olympia Trading Estate, Coburg Road, Wood Green,
London N22 6TZ, England.

First edition published in 1984 by Harper & Row, Publishers.
First Alyson edition: April 1998

02 01 00 99 98   10 9 8 7 6 5 4 3 2 1

ISBN 1-55583-407-8
(Previously published with ISBN 0-06-091178-6)

Grateful acknowledgment is made for permission to reprint:

"In Time of Warhol" by Quentin Crisp, © 1975 by Punch/Rothco. "Summer Exhibition" by Quentin Crisp, © 1978 by Punch/Rothco. "Australia and How to Cure It" by Quentin Crisp, © 1978 by Punch/Rothco. All of these first appeared in *Punch.*

"On Riding Trains," excerpted from "Riding with a Stiff Upper Lip," by Quentin Crisp, first appeared in *The New York Times.* © 1983 by The New York Times Company. Reprinted by permission.

"I Visit the Colonies," "Bloomingdale's vs. Harrods," "On Being English in New York" excerpted from "I Visit the Colonies," by Quentin Crisp. First appeared in *New York* magazine. Reprinted with the permission of *New York* magazine.

"Miss Garland," "*Frances,*" "*The Hunger,*" and "*Ernesto*" excerpted from *Christopher Street* magazine. Reprinted by permission of That New Magazine Inc., publishers of *Christopher Street* magazine.

"Mr. Crisp's Record of Employment" (excluding "The Declining Nude") excerpted from *The Naked Civil Servant* by Quentin Crisp. © 1968 by Quentin Crisp. Reprinted by arrangement with New American Library, New York, New York.

To Connie Clausen

CONTENTS

PART ONE

PART TWO

PART THREE

PART FOUR

PART FIVE

PART SIX

PART SEVEN

PART EIGHT

PART NINE

The joy in compiling *The Wit and Wisdom of Quentin Crisp* came not only because of the wealth of material at my disposal but because Mr. Crisp is one of those rare people who speak as they write. Transcribing tapes, whether of conversations I had with him in his tiny room on the Lower East Side of Manhattan or of one of his performances, in a packed auditorium in New Orleans, was an extraordinary experience: the words fell onto the page as gracefully as they had been spoken.

Mr. Crisp's style and personality are the results of a lifetime of conscious choice and meticulous honing. He has created himself. His words–written or spoken–are the product of this creation. Mr. Crisp believes that by nature we are nothing, by nurture everything, and while his own modesty would prevent him from saying so, he is a most vivid example of how fully developed a human being can become through careful self-nurturing.

But there is far more to Mr. Crisp than carefully constructed artifice. Style and sincerity are the same thing in him (as he says they must be in any true stylist), and his incisive opinions and observations are completely served by the wit and grace with which they are expressed. You may find yourself falling off a chair laughing at a "Crispism," but you'll haul yourself back up astonished at what you've learned.

The Wit and Wisdom of Quentin Crisp offers a wide sampling from such disparate publications as *Christopher Street, The New York Times, The Movies, After Dark, New York* magazine, and *Punch.* I've borrowed chunks from his brilliant *How to Have a Life-Style* because it contains some of the most illuminating critical writing (also some of his funniest). Although it is in print, I have also excerpted from his classic autobiography, *The Naked Civil Servant,* since no collection of Crisp could justifiably appear without selections from the book that first revealed him to an unsuspecting world. There is also the "live" Quentin Crisp, thoughtful in extended conversation, startling in his extemporaneous responses to question asked him by audiences at performances.

Mr. Crisp comes across here as a commentator, an entertainer, a stylist, but also an instructor. His mission is to show us, via a varied road map—a "journey to the interior"—how to be happy. There is little choice but to take a look inside, Mr. Crisp tells us, if happiness is our goal: "If to look upward is vain because, to put it politely, You-Know-Who is resting, and to gaze about us is unbearable, where else is there to look but within?"

Guy Kettelhack

QUENTIN CRISP ON QUENTIN CRISP

Quentin Crisp was reluctantly born on Christmas Day in 1908. To his dismay, he found himself to be the son of middle-class, middlebrow, middling parents who lived in Sutton, a suburb of London, England. After an uneventful childhood, he was sent, between the ages of 14 and 18, to a school in Derbyshire which was like a cross between a monastery and a prison. There he learned nothing that could ever be useful to him in adulthood except how to bear injustice. His ignorance of everything but this and his ambiguous appearance made a career impossible except in the arts. He therefore became an illustrator and a designer of book covers. When he could no longer bear constantly being given the sack, he tried freelancing. From time to time he wrote books on an assortment of subjects—on lettering (a craft which he had never mastered), on window dressing, on the Ministry of Labour (with which, at that time, he had never had any connection except as an applicant for the dole).

At length, almost by chance, he stood in for a friend who was an art school model, and finding that the effort did not cause him to collapse, he took up posing as a career. With this way of life he struggled on for 35 years. In the middle 1960s, on a British radio channel to which no one listens, he uttered a few words that led to his being invited to write his autobiography. The synopsis of this proposed work caused the man who had commissioned it to faint dead away, but another firm, Jonathan Cape, agreed to publish it in 1968. This was an offer that Mr. Crisp could not refuse, because he was paid in advance.

Looking back, the press likes to refer to the book as "a best-seller at the time." It was no such thing. It received respectful reviews, sold about 3,500 copies, and caused no sensation whatsoever until it was translated into a television scenario by Mr. Mackie, who then, for four long, dark years, ran hatless through the streets of London trying to nag producers into making it into a movie. He failed.

Ultimately, forced by fatigue to lower his sights, Mr. Mackie cajoled Thames Television into making his script into a television play. In this new, improved form, *The Naked Civil Servant* was well-received–even by critics. Their approbation caused awards to be sprinkled like confetti upon Mr. John Hurt, who played the leading part in it, on its director, Mr. Gold, on its production team, headed by Miss Lambert, and on Mr. Mackie. This program has been shown three times in England and broadcast in Australia, New Zealand, Canada, America, and in various European countries. No credit for the excellence of this play is due to Mr. Crisp; he is merely the raw material from which it is made.

Nevertheless, a certain amount of curiosity about the subject of such a sensational autobiography has prompted producers to present him in a variety of ventures so that the world might have the opportunity of affirming his existence, of hearing what he has to say, and of asking him questions. In the last five years he has visited a number of towns and cities in England and Australia and appeared at the Edinburgh and Belfast festivals. He made his off-Broadway debut in *An Evening with Quentin Crisp* in 1978 and has since been seen by New York audiences as Lady Bracknell in *The Importance of Being Earnest* at the Soho Repertory Theatre.

Upon becoming a resident alien of the United States in 1981, he moved to New York City, vowing never to leave. Until very recently, Mr. Crisp found it difficult to believe in abroad. It seemed too remote to anyone who had lived for 38 years in one room in Chelsea—incidentally, without ever cleaning it. In the winter of his life, he describes himself on his income tax forms as a retired waif. Having been unsuccessfully an artist, a teacher of tap dancing, an occasional writer, and a minor televisionary, he is now an old-age pensioner—a career at which he can hardly fail. In spite of all this, he has the nerve to preach on the subject of life-style and claims with the aid of it to be able to cure you of your excessive freedom, which he deems to be the cause of the world's ills. These public appearances are his humble attempt to thank the human race for having to some extent revised the condemnatory opinion it has held of him for so long.

PART ONE

Style

In Soho–the hooligan district of London–there lived a woman known to her fellow hooligans as the Countess. She suffered from almost all the ill effects of undernourishment and exposure to inclement weather. She had no fixed address and no means of support and her body was bent double from a lifelong habit of looking into trash cans to see if she could find something she could possibly sell to a kind friend or, if not, that she herself might be able to use.

One day, in a garbage can in the most expensive part of London, she found a complete backless, beaded dress. She longed for night to fall so that she could nip into a dark doorway and try it on, but by about half past 6 her patience was worn out. It was barely dusk, but she went into a churchyard in the middle of London and there she proceeded to take off her clothes. This caused a crowd to collect, and the crowd caused a policeman to collect.

The next day, in court, when the magistrate said, "...and what exactly were you doing, stripping among the dead?" she replied, "I was doing what any woman would be doing at that hour–changing for dinner."

Style and . . .

. . . IDENTITY

Style, in the broadest sense of all, is consciousness.

Most people are at present content to cherish their mere identity. This is not enough. Our identity is just a group of ill-assorted characteristics that we happen to be born with. Like our fingerprints, if they are noticed at all, they will almost certainly be used against us.

You have to polish up your raw identity into a life-style so that you can barter with the outside world for what you want. This polishing process makes your life so formal that by comparison the life of a Trappist monk is an orgy.

The search for a life-style involves a journey to the interior. This is not altogether a pleasant experience, because you not only have to take stock of what you consider your assets but also have to take a long look at what your friends call "the trouble with you." Nevertheless, the journey is worth making. Indeed, we might say that the whole purpose of existence is to reconcile the glowing opinion we have of ourselves with the terrible things other people say about us.

If, when you peer into your soul, you find that you are ordinary, then ordinary is what you must remain, but you must be so ordinary that you can imagine someone saying, "Come to my party and bring your humdrum friend," and everyone knowing that he meant you.

Style and...

. . . TELEVISION

It used to be thought that only the rich and famous needed style. Television has changed all that. We can now see that there are people in our society who can earn vast sums of money, become the world's sweethearts, be photographed at airports, and be known by name to hotel proprietors, without displaying talent of any kind.

This phenomenon cannot be regarded as an unmixed blessing. Television is certainly to blame for contributing to the madness of young people by bombarding their consciences with the lurid spectacle of worldwide injustice. Even so it would be futile and, worse, styleless to attempt to limit its activities.

At the very least it should be treated like Chinese rape. As it is inevitable, we should relax and enjoy its influence upon our lives. This attitude would at least have the effect of calling the bluff of newscasters. The spreading of shocking news is not a denunciation of war and similar so-called evils. It is a way of selling television sets. It is a parallel activity with the making of pornographic films. The publicity for such movies is pseudopuritanical, but the audience is invariably pleased to see that debauchery fills the screen for nine tenths of the film's showing time, at the end of which retribution gets to work faster than a clip joint warned that there is going to be a raid.

An even more stylish method of dealing with rape is not merely to consent but sexually to assault the rapist. As Noël Coward has said, television is not a thing to watch. It is a thing to be on. This is what many people think, but they do not do enough about it. Like Mr. Macbeth (surely the most styleless Scotsman to wear kilts), what they would highly that would they genteelly. This will not do.

Any one of us, be he ever so humble, may find himself "on," and woe to him if he is not prepared with his own style. He may otherwise find himself simpering and answering some impertinent interviewer's questions with "Uh-uh-uh," when in fact he knows, as most of us do, that he has fascinating opinions about every subject under the sun.

Already, of course, we are being affected by television in the conduct of our daily lives without fully realizing it. Ten years ago, a housewife, interrupted in her shopping by a reporter and asked what she thought of the Common Market, would have clapped her hand to her lips, giggled a little, and mumbled that she supposed it was all right. Today it is to be hoped that the same woman in the same situation would spot the camera in a second, smile graciously at it, and drawing a deep but covert breath, would begin, "While on the one hand certain superficial historians might say…"

In this respect the influence of television is entirely good, but we must do more than think of it as an enemy against whose intermittent stares we must brace ourselves. We must welcome its interest and rise joyfully to its challenge by taking our life-style with us wherever we go. It provides us with the ideal means of swotting up our stagecraft. Many confrontations and interviews are stored up for showing at a later date–possibly at several later dates–and this enables us to see ourselves not, mercifully, as others see us, which is always worse than we really are, but as the camera sees us, which may be a more nearly unbiased view. Thus we have an advantage that was once available only to movie actors, who every evening see the rushes of their day's work so that errors can be observed and corrected.

Looked at from the front, a television screen appears to be a lighted rectangle full of celebrities and other disasters. Seen from behind, it is an arid waste in which, like farmers in a dust bowl, broadcasters and producers dig for something–anything–on which to feed their bleating flocks.

Television is inextricably woven into our lives, and television has so much spare time that everybody will be on it in the end.

Style and . . .

. . . PRIVACY

Mr. Richard Burton and Miss Elizabeth Taylor (who are so great that both of them even brought style to marriage) once complained openly that the newsmen in Italy seemed likely at any moment to photograph one or the other of them in the bathroom. The way to deal with this problem (if it is one) is not to build a higher wall around the house but to learn to urinate with style.

If machines come into existence which can collect and tabulate all the relevant facts about everyone in Britain and America and cram them all into a space the size of a telephone booth, it will be done. And what is more, when the information has been gathered, it will be used.

What else has it been gathered for?

By 1984 there will be a governmental and lidless eye gazing down at the occupant of every room in every city in our part of the world. This prospect causes some people to feel positively suicidal. Why? At present many of us spend hours of every evening waltzing round the town without, to our chagrin, causing the slightest stir. When fatigue prevents us from staying out a moment longer, we return home, rip off our eyelashes, and embrace defeat. In a few years' time, however, our anguish will be over. Even at home we shall feel we are worth watching. Margaret or Ronnie will care.

Style and . . .

. . . EDUCATION

When I was a child, I never thought as a child. I subscribed meekly to my parents' idea that a good education was a protracted one. Scholarship seemed to them to be a weapon for use against a hostile world, and I often heard my mother nagging my father to equip me with it. Later there was a regrouping of forces. "Operation Pelican" set in. This consisted of their uniting to reproach me with the enormity of my school fees. This happened shortly before I left college.

Then my views on education underwent their first drastic change. The scales fell from my eyes, and I saw the whole system as a giant extractor in which the government squeezed from its slaves whatever elemental juices they might contain in the hope of coming across something upon which it could feed.

Things have changed once again since then. I now realize that education is a last wild effort on the part of the authorities to prevent an overdose of leisure from driving the world mad. Learning is no longer an improver; it is merely the most expensive time filler the world has ever known.

Evening classes are of use only if you learn to sing and dance, because these are activities the results of which the student takes out into the world with him and wears like a crown. People who have learned to sing, whether they ever sing professionally or not, will always have richer, rounder voices; people who have learned to dance will always have bigger, bolder movements—but of what use are pottery and basket weaving? Once the doors of the evening institute clang behind you, you're where you started. If on the way home you were to become involved in an argument with a stranger at a bus stop, you might find yourself saying, "Well, I can't express myself; you'll have to come and see my baskets."

Style and . . .

. . . POLITICS, WAR, AND REVOLUTION

Politics is the art of making the inevitable appear to be a matter of wise human choice.

The great political stylist was Mrs. Perón. I don't know if many people realize in what a personal and at the same time pervasive way she ruled her kingdom. In England, spelling primers begin with the words "The cat sat on the mat." No wonder literacy is at a low ebb, when the first glimpse of it is this banal and even distasteful piece of information. But in Argentina, spelling books begin with "I love Evita."

The crowning moment of her entire career was when she

stood up in her box in the opera house in Buenos Aires and made a speech. She lifted her hands to the crowd, and as she did so, with a sound like railway trucks in a siding, the diamond bracelets slid down from her wrists. When the expensive clatter had died away, her speech began, "We, the shirtless…"

You may not believe in Mrs. Perón, but the Argentineans did. So much so that when she died they petitioned the Pope to make her a saint. His Holiness declined; but if he'd consented, what a triumph for style *that* would have been! A double fox stole, ankle-strap shoes, and eternal life. Nobody's ever had that.

The young have not the means to cure the ills of the world: they can only protest—the more angrily because it can be seen that their action is futile. It is years since marchers stopped impeding the normal flow of traffic between Aldermaston and Trafalgar Square, and still nuclear bombs are tested and still more armaments pile up.

To make matters even more pathetic, half the time the world-savers are crying out against situations that are not ills at all. War is the most obvious of these. No less an authority than Sir Edmund Leach, the social anthropologist, states that to live under the perpetual threat of invasion is normal and almost certainly salutary.

We all knew it was normal. Even Walt Disney, the Archdeacon of Twee, did not try to bury this fact beneath a heap of sugar. In none of his nature films was there ever a single chipmunk that ate his lunch in peace. After seeing any of these movies, one felt that possibly small animals die as often from ulcers as from enemy activity.

To say that war is salutary is another matter. The statement requires an explanation, and this Sir Edmund is prepared to give on behalf of the majority. It increases the solidarity of nations, he says, and reaffirms boundaries. This last remark is the first flash of style to illumine the landscape in a long time. It is another and much more daring way of saying that without a frame there can be no satisfactory picture.

It also makes clear that to great modern thinkers human life is no longer sacred. We should have known that this would be so. Nothing except diamonds is above the law of scarcity value.

Politics are really the same everywhere. Just as teaching is for teachers, politics are for politicians. Once you've grasped that, you understand the whole situation. Politics are a way in which certain people with certain gifts project themselves onto the world.

Never in the history of the world has the currency of any country come to be worth more. So when you become the king, the president, the prime minister, you have to find a way of telling me why everything in the shops has got more expensive, and while you tell me, you have got to smile.

❖   ❖   ❖

Children grow up thinking that all the world is in perpetual violent turmoil, and this means that they grow up with this terrible feeling that the world has been mismanaged by their parents, and that they must change it. Therefore they either take jobs where they can opt out entirely; or have the view that they should all go out to the middle of Biafra, and this to my mind is bad.

There are situations which cannot be resolved; there are questions for which there are no answers, and if you don't accept this, then you will rapidly develop a police mentality. You will search for culprits, you will tear up contradictory evidence, and you will push people around until they are in easily labeled and easily controlled blocs. And I think some way must be found of getting the children to realize they live in a imperfect world, that there are no political systems which will make a difference. In fact, I would try and get children to see that politics is a complete waste of time.

Style and . . .

. . . **ACTING**

An actor's kingdom is divided into three provinces–the dressing room, the rehearsal room, and the stage. Everything else is unreal. We must partition our lives in exactly the same way. Our homes are sometimes dressing rooms and at other times rehearsal rooms; all the world's our stage. Ideally, when the place where we live is our dressing room, we must use it only for preparing to "go on stage" or as an area in which to relax. The search for a life-style will occupy a great deal of your day. It would therefore be wise not to waste time on domestic rituals. It is quite unnecessary to clean the place where you live, because after four years the dirt doesn't become any worse. It is just a question of not losing your nerve.

Stage people find it difficult to distinguish between their private lives and whatever part they are playing in the theater. But what am I saying? They flatly refuse to make the slightest effort to separate them. So when the theater of certainty prevailed, they were certain; when plays were about dukes and duchesses, they were duchessy. During the '20s an actress could be seen by all the world to be very different from an ordinary mortal. Not only at the stage door but wherever she went she was—she arranged to be—an object of absorbing interest. She had a face like an egg to which cosmetics had been applied, and all her movements were operatic. On taking a seat in a public vehicle she crossed her legs so that one shin was almost horizontal and her instep painfully arched. Then she spread the ruching on her dress so that it covered the knees of at least two gentlemen on either side of her and, in tones like the sound of Big Ben, remarked, "These trains are absolute hell."

These antics were to her what a blue apron was to a butcher.

That Mme. Bernhardt was called "The Divine Sarah" we may discount. She was so named not because of her skill but because of her nationality. A race of people so grossly materialistic as the French must from time to time utter spiritual sighs. It is a kind of moral balance of payments. Nevertheless, Mme. Bernhardt was at one time a star by comparison with whom most experts found all other tragediennes wanting. After reading the works of Mr. James Agate one feels unfit to pass judgment on any subject whatsoever if one never saw Mme. Bernhardt.

Other critics have been less ecstatic. Seeing her in *Hamlet*, Sir Max Beerbohm said that if she had possessed a sense of humor she would never have taken the part in the first place. This is only one man's opinion, but evidence can be adduced which cannot be gainsaid. There is in existence a record of her voice. The poor quality of the reproduction and the age of the disc may have lessened the sonority of her speech, but the monotony of her delivery, the lack of range and of rubato, are obvious for all to hear. In the entire recitation, the tears never leave her throat.

Even more damning is a movie made of Mme. Bernhardt in the death scene from *Camille*. I have witnessed a screening of this at the National Film Theatre. Awkwardly held at arm's length by Armand as though she were a firecracker (which, in a way, she was), she half sat, half lay on a couch, wearing a minimum-risk nightdress, clown's makeup, and hair that looked as though she had found it under the bed. Though someone must surely have told her that the picture was silent, the moment the cameras began to turn, her black lips started to gibber and twitch faster than those of a policeman giving corrupt evidence, and, sometimes in unison and sometimes in succession, her arms shot out to punch the air before returning after each sortie to strike her a massive blow in the chest. Then, as suddenly as all this galvanic activity had begun, it stopped. Her head fell forward and one arm swung down beside the couch like the limb of a rag doll.

I am a self-confessed philistine, but I was not alone in rejecting at once the myth of Mme. Bernhardt's histrionic ability. As everybody knows, almost no one who is not a Master of Arts and does not live in the cheese and wine belt of Hampstead can gain admission to the National Film Theatre. Yet when this piece of film was shown, the entire house choked with mirth. A man sitting near me became so convulsed with merriment that he fell out of his seat into the aisle and lay there with his feet waving in the air like a supine wood louse.

From all this we may conclude that it was not by means of what she did on the stage that Mme. Bernhardt ruled France. She brought the nation to its knees by what she did with the rest of her time–by spending her nights in her coffin and her days surrounded by a cheetah, a monkey, a parrot, four dogs, and M. Gustave Doré.

The same writer who accused Mme. Bernhardt of lacking humor praised her autobiography for having that very quality. Perhaps in this apparent contradiction lies one of the secrets of life-style. An element of self-mockery should always be woven into our attitude toward our description of our past behavior, but should never prevent us from flinging ourselves with total commitment into the present and making it a backcloth for our most extravagant gesture.

Style and . . .

. . . ATHLETICS

A person who is preparing his life-style should avoid playing even the mildest of games if they do not constitute a part of that style. For one thing, he might not win; and for another, competition of any kind encourages a man to make comparisons between himself and other people, which is a completely misguided activity of mind.

However, all this said, physical training is important. Indeed, it is the keystone of a happy life. Slow, controlled rituals performed in private–with even the breathing deliberate–are recommended as part of a stylist's training. For a more detailed description of these exercises, I would recommend the reading of books on yoga were it not for the fact that beyond Hatha Yoga lie other, more mysterious strata of this cult. The study of these leads almost inevitably to trouble with the infinite. It may be true that preoccupation with time has been the downfall of Western man, but it can also be argued that conjecture about eternity is a waste of time.

Style and . . .

. . . C R I M E

In modern life a stylist does not even need virtue. It is no longer necessary to be an object of public veneration or even affection. He can be the focus of contempt or even downright hatred. Illustrations of this abound. As a test of whether you are in touch with somebody, being loved can never be a patch on being murdered. That's when somebody really has risked his life for you. If you have chosen depravity as the fluid in which you will suspend your monstrous ego, then you have the most wonderful examples before you–or rather behind you, because most of the ones we can best identify are in history.

M. Gilles de Rais murdered at least 140 boys in a lifetime. Numbers are not style, but it's difficult not to be impressed. He was a nobleman, and the projection of his life-style was made easy for him by the fact that, while he was rich and owned more than one castle, most people in France were so poor that whole families of peasants left their homes to wander about the countryside in search of food much as, according to Comrade Boris Pasternak, the Russian bourgeoisie did during the early days of the Revolution. M. de Rais caused it to be known that he was not only wealthy but also an extremely religious man who maintained a large boys' choir in his castle in Tiffauges. This was a way of luring into his grasp victims of the age that suited his tastes. When the boys arrived, hoping to become part of the choir, he murdered them and ravished them while they were dying or, if they died quickly, when they were dead.

I expect that rape and murder, either separately or mixed together, fill the fantasies of most men and all stylists. They are the supreme acts of ascendancy over others; they yield the only moments when a man is certain beyond all doubt that his message has been received. Of the few who live out these dreams, some preface rape with murder so as to avoid embracing a partner who might criticize their technique.

M. de Rais was a very different manner of man. He occasionally gave select ravishment parties. He would never have done this if he had been physically inadequate. Orgies are for sexual athletes.

After a while not even a pinch of exhibitionism could prevent his desire from outrunning his delight. He took to riding into the countryside and hunting down his little friends. (Here once again we see the strong connection between crime and sport.) In these sorties he was accompanied by a certain M. de Sillé, not so much, I feel, because he needed help as in order to have his prowess in the field admired by his peers.

When he was finally brought to trial, it was for quite another offense, but by this time rumors about his life-style had begun to spread across the land. On a journey through France he had murdered a boy while staying at an inn, and this child had parents who noticed his disappearance.

If proof were needed that style engenders style, it could be found in accounts of M. de Rais's trial. His confession was so long and so lurid that the Bishop of Nantes ordered the face of the crucifix on the wall behind him to be covered. Moreover, style was not confined to the courtroom. People came from far and wide throughout France to pray for his soul. Some of these people were the parents of the children he had murdered. If this is not style, it is at least gesture on a national scale, all brought about by one man.

At the last M. de Rais cried out, "I am redeemable." Into what shade is the whole of Mr. Oscar Wilde's *De Profundis* flung by this single sentence!

The police, who can hardly be expected to approve of style, tell us that with the passage of time criminals become careless–that in the end they slip up. It seems to me more likely that they grow increasingly daring. There have been burglars who fed the housewife's cat and bandits who kissed the ladies in the plundered coach. These are obvious instances of artists extending their style, but almost all crooks from petty thieves to Mr. Jack the Ripper stamp their crimes with their own pattern. In spite of everything, they wish their identity to be recognized. In this respect the most satisfactory life of crime was lived by highwaymen like Mr. Dick Turpin, who were known to many and revered by some for years before they were finally caught. If we think of a life of crime as a way of making something of ourselves, then we see at once that detection is not a piece of bad luck but a consummation.

Penology is another sphere of human activity which has suffered the sad homogenizing effect of time. We have now reached a state of affairs in which, if you steal a sufficiently large sum of money or murder a small enough person, you are given the same sentence. In Mr. Turpin's day the crowning moment of a criminal's life was his public execution. Compared with this, what an anticlimactic end it was to shuffle toward the noose in the presence of a mere handful of hardened, sanctimonious officials! Now murder has had even more of its style wrested from it by the abolition of capital punishment. If this seems a heartless observation, it should be remembered that it was not trapeze artists who wanted the use of the safety net made compulsory. It was a group of busybodies who wished to rob these performers of the most effective element of their life-style.

To a religious person, though it disobeys the teaching of the Old Testament, the abolition of hanging accords with the principles of the New. It allows the sinner time to repent—possibly even to atone. This is the most that can be said for it. Life imprisonment robs detective fiction of its formality and murder of its special quality. It is not a merciful sentence, though it may seem to be. Mr. Dostoyevsky has told the world his thoughts as he stood before the executioners. If he had at that moment been offered as an alternative to immediate death the chance to live the rest of his natural life on a ledge a foot wide over a bottomless abyss, he would have chosen it. This only means that the body prefers, always tries, to save itself. To the mind, life at any cost is not always preferable. If many free men wish for and some bring about their own death, a man with an eternity of prison ahead of him must think of suicide every day. Of capital punishment it could at least be said that it saved a man from the weakest elements of his own nature.

Crime has in common with sport that it fulfills every man's

fantasy of plunging into the midst of terrible danger and sur-
viving. Mr. Stirling Moss once said (and who should have
known better than a racing car driver?) that the best way to
live is "flat out with every decision mattering"—as though the
whole of life were the Grand Prix. In such circumstances as
these, the stylist's ideal of living in the continuous present
throughout his body is not just a vague dream of perfection;
it is an immediate and total necessity. On the racetrack, one
must do this or die.

MATING PLUMAGE

With eyes aflame and hands clasping a plastic molecule to
his palpitating bosom, Dr. Jacob Bronowski once said on television, "The arrow of time points always in the direction of
diminishing difference." I seem to remember that he was
speaking of some aspect of physics, but his law governs all
human experience.

As each distinction in English life disappears, its departure
has some effect upon what men wear.

The first frontier to be obliterated was that which divided nations. To wear a beret ceased to give assurance that
you were French or even wished that you were; to stumble
about in clogs no longer signified that you came from Hol-
land. For the young of all countries, fancy dress became national costume.

The next wall to crumble was that which separated classes. A kind of "trianonism" set in. Even if you invited the sons
of peerage to dinner, they arrived in jeans or boiler suits as

though you had asked them to help you paint your ceilings. These changes occurred almost without comment.

Then all visible differences between the sexes vanished: not only do heterosexual couples now wear similar clothes; their stock of garments is held in common. On waking in the morning, a modern husband says to his wife, "If you will not be needing them, I think I'll try the mink-edged jeans." This attitude has caused an outcry—at least among the middle-aged. No wonder. It is a sure sign that our civilization is at an end.

I am not at all surprised that this convergence has taken place; on the contrary, I am amazed that it has been so long in arriving.

When you glance through *A Man's Book,* compiled by Miss Waller from magazine articles of the '20s and '30s, you realize that never a year went by without some fashion journal remarking on the trend away from uniform drabness (at that time an accepted symbol of well-bred maleness) to something less rigid in contour and brighter in color. In 1926 Mr. Bennett went to the Royal Academy's Summer Exhibition in a brown bowler; another year, the Prince of Wales, that decade's paragon of style, attended a race meeting in a blue shirt. Where, one asked oneself, would it all end?

In 1929 the Dress Reform Club came into being. Some of its members proposed replacing trousers with kilts. It is true that these and other such changes—all recommended in the interests of comfort or hygiene—were the ideas of aged cranks and never taken seriously by younger men. Nevertheless, stitch by stitch, a gusset at a time, while women's fashions darted this way and that, frequently recrossing their own path like travelers lost in snow, men's appearance crept steadily toward the barbed wire that guarded the difference between the sexes.

So far Dr. Bronowski has been proved right; but there is another law besides his which must also be obeyed.

If you force a plant into a pot too small for its roots, it will flower in one last desperate effort to propagate its species. This is the position in which the human race now finds itself. Our planet has become too small for us. Therefore, while ecologists and even governments implore us to restrain our creative impulses, we are becoming sexier. This development is more apparent in men's than in women's clothing.

In the '20s girls wanted to marry at all costs. To many, this was their only chance of winning financial security. Already it was known that wedlock was not a stable condition. Divorce was all the rage, but women knew that, though marriage is for a little while, alimony is forever. With this in mind, they pursued prospective mates who looked like bankers. Since then young ladies' aims have altered; they have found easier ways to earn a living than marriage. They now search for lovers rather than husbands. Men can look less reliable, more romantic. This situation is reinforced by another fact.

Fifty years ago a music hall song warned us that there were in England 50 million surplus women making surplus eyes. Men could afford to look and to be boring. That ration no longer prevails. The Second World War was unlike the first in the same way that a sniper's bullet differs from buckshot. In1940 not only soldiers but people of both sexes, and people of all ages, and from every class were given an opportunity to die. The bombs were a great leveler. Without even knowing why, boys, because of their superfluity, have now adopted more self-consciously colorful mating plumage.

In the ornithological world this ruse works more wonders than the offer of a diamond bracelet, but among humans there are harmful side effects. Only very young girls are willing to swoon over a vain man. More mature women fear that they may lose the fight for the mirror.

Physical vanity is still secretly considered to be a feminine vice and is therefore unattractive to most women. While becoming more flamboyant, men's attire must be in a poorer state of repair and must be obviously masculine. The entire relationship between the sexes has become more explicit. Women toy with the idea of topless dresses, and men wear trousers so tight that you can see what they are thinking.

The codpiece is on its way.

In the days when our love life was in the hands of the poets, suits were designed to flatter the male physique and to hide what were considered its less decorous features. This will never be so again.

Mr. Andy Warhol tells us that, after makeup, clothes make the man. It doesn't seem at all unlikely that soon cosmetics will be in common use among men, but their purposes will not be to make us look younger or healthier. The most prophetic film of recent years was undoubtedly *A Clockwork Orange;* every day another of its prognostications is fulfilled. In that movie the hero wore false lashes above and below one eye and left the other naked. In time to come, whatever we put on ourselves will only be there to mock the human frame. The ship of fashion has foundered, with all souls lost off Punk Rock.

Dressing is now an act of revenge against our bodies because they have failed to provide us with that perpetual unalloyed pleasure promised by the pornographers.

CODA

It's no good running a pig farm for 30 years while saying, "I was meant to be a ballet dancer." By that time the pigs are your style.

PART TWO

In which Mr. Crisp explains

SEX, LOVE, ROMANCE,
& MARRIAGE

Live alone.

The continued propinquity of another human being cramps the style after a time unless that person is somebody you think you love. Then the burden becomes intolerable at once. This may seem to be carrying monasticism to unbearable extremes, but dry your tears. What is frowned upon is cohabitation rather than sex.

If sex were still a private matter, it would require little or no mention. This, alas, is not the case. Recently it has been given a great deal of uncoverage in the press, on television, and in the movies. The people who raise the loudest and most persistent objection to this are the moralists. Stylists can never concern themselves with ethics, but they too cannot help forming opinions about excessive sexual license as about any other misuse of freedom. In becoming a public pastime and a topic for incessant conversation, sex has not increased its style. Indeed, much of what it formerly possessed it has lost.

Instant sex is a time- and labor-saving device, but as leisure and energy are what we now have to excess, this is no recommendation. For flavor it will never supersede unpleasant truths that the permissive society has brought to light. We are now all dangerously aware that sexual intercourse is a bit of a bore. What kept the "divine woman" lark going for all those long, dark centuries was not an unquenchable erection but romance. If this had not been so, how could the troubadours of the Middle Ages have managed to hog all that peak-hour viewing time?

Romance was the style in sex.

I once saw a movie in which Mary Astor promised her daughter a rich, full life. She did not give a list of ingredients. I would say they were innocence, wonder, romance, debauchery, indiscretion, and death, but *in that order.*

It used to be said of America that she had passed from barbarism to decadence without ever becoming civilized. I would say that modern adolescents went from innocence to debauchery without ever knowing romance, but while inveighing against the permissive society I would not wish to be thought mingling my squeaks with those of Mrs. Mary White Mouse, England's local arbiter of television morality. I differ from her in that I do not think there is a pin to choose between innocence and debauchery. I complain merely because I feel that everyone, like a passenger on a luxury liner, should be allowed to work his way through the whole menu even if it makes him sick. The young are debarred from doing this. After decadence there can be no civilization; after debauchery, no romance.

To replace romance we are now offered every possible kind of kinkiness. It is not a satisfactory substitute. What is wrong with pornography is that it is a successful attempt to sell sex for more than it is worth. To give a peripheral example, let me ask how it is that those Swedish girls who, with their golden muscles rippling and their finespun hair afloat, are forever running naked through the woods never happen to tread on a thistle—or worse. If we go deeper into the subject, we find that if ever we compare with those of other readers our impressions of a pornographic book, someone always remarks of the hero, "He must have been inexhaustible."

But most real live men are not inexhaustible. The price that may have to be paid for sexual activity on a massive scale includes nervous prostration, syphilis, unwanted pregnancy, social, emotional, and financial entanglement. None of these items is listed in the catalogue.

Far be it from me to advocate a return to "family" entertainment. The word "family" as used in this phrase describes a dream unit presided over by a daughter's idea of a father, kept spick-and-span by a son's idea of a mother, and romped in (innocently) by a parent's idea of children. In fact, if someone were to set up a production in which Miss Bette Davis was directed by Mr. Roman Polanski, it could not express to the full the pent-up violence and depravity of a single day in the life of the average family. On the other hand, pornography is no more satisfying. As the actor and director Mr. Bryan Forbes has said, so far from being entertaining, it is depressing—especially to those who take it most seriously, the sexually inadequate. There is a vision of shimmering mockery before the bulging eyes of people who suffer from some degree of impotence. It tells them that if only they could have sexual intercourse with a red-haired Japanese girl on a green motorbike on a Wednesday, everything would be different. Then they would experience some immeasurable delight of which circumstances have so far deprived them. Alas, it is a mirage! It is not possible in reality to extort from sexual activity more than your nervous system will stand. Man's reach exceeds his grasp, or what is Hades for?

It is especially the young who do not seem to know this. They stagger along the primrose path of pleasure, mistakenly believing that it leads to happiness, until their nerves are frayed to bits. This is partly the reason why there are few people between the ages of 15 and 25 who do not have to be waked every morning with stimulants in order that they may drift through the day on sedatives.

Children overeat. Everyone who has dealt with young children knows that infants cry as often from bewilderment at too wide a choice as they do from frustration. Mr. Peter Fonda says that choice is a form of imprisonment rather than a kind of freedom. It was naughty of him to say this. It is a half-truth. It is not choice but indecision that is inhibiting.

When I inveigh against both eternal love and the striving for equality, I am not trying to inhibit anyone's sex life. I merely wish to snatch the straw from every woman's beak and prevent her from nesting. If two people share a territory, ultimately they will be left with only the things about which they disagree. If a man gets up at 6 every morning and his wife does the same, within a fortnight he will be saying, "Isn't it fortunate; we agree." If, on the other hand, he likes the soap to be on the right side of the washbasin and his wife prefers it on the left, they are heading for a divorce. Their friends will exclaim, "You're getting divorced over a cake of soap?" They do not realize that he had to move it every day.

Q: Since people persist in getting married, what would your advice be to them?

A: Do not expect that you will be happy. Do not enter a marriage thinking this is the way in which I will be happy. If you do that you are making use of your partner. You must enter into a marriage knowing that you are sacrificing yourself. You must say, "I feel I have all sorts of things to give to a relationship, and I will find somebody to whom I can give them. And I only expect to die fulfilled—not happy—that I have done what little I could do."

Q: So it is possible to be fulfilled in marriage?

A: If your view is that your style—your image—is to be self-sacrificing, and if you feel you have an infinite capacity for sacrificing yourself, then you may think: Will I go to India to feed the starving, or to Crimea to bind up the wounds of the injured—or will I just get married?

If I were asked to describe the difference between the sexes in the gay world, I would say that the men wanted to be amused; the girls sought vindication.

I urgently feel that if gay people want to be happy, they must vacate their secret world; they must stop frightening not only the horses but also their riders. They must recognize that it is in the very nature of integration that you cannot fight for it. You can only wait.

Q: Is "butchness" the style now for gay men?

A: It is a fashion. You understand when I use the word "style," I am not speaking of fashion. Fashion is *instead* of style. When you don't know who you are, then you consult the papers. There is a restaurant in New York where there isn't a woman in sight and everyone there is wearing tractor boots, preruined jeans, kitchen-tablecloth shirts, and small mustaches. The only way you know you haven't strayed into the canteen of a building site is that they're all so clean. They look marvelous, but it can't be *true* of all of them. In England manliness has progressed further and into the realm of cruelty. There are bars in England where the men wear boots up to here and gloves up to here and jackets out to there and they have remembered to carry their crash helmets under their arms. They come by bus.

Q: Does the homosexual's life-style of a survivor have anything to teach other people?

A: Oh, yes. They will have the burden and the enjoyment of being survivors, of being outside and of being aware that every day that they live is a kind of triumph. And this they should cling on to. They should make no effort to try and join society. They should stay right where they are and give their name and serial number and wait for society to form itself around them. Because it certainly will.

The happiest moments in any affair take place after the loved one has learned to accommodate the lover and before the maddening personality of either party has emerged like a jagged rock from the receding tides of lust and curiosity. Even then, for homosexual men complete fulfillment is very rare. Where only sensation and frequency of sensation are the point, monotony rapidly leads to experimental extremes in the hope that variety of circumstances will add spice to the chore of several orgasms a day, but in fact, sex at the back of the classroom or in an elevator between the mezzanine and the second floor is more enjoyable in the recounting at parties than at the time when it was experienced. Those who avoid these smash-and-grab raids are really hardly interested in physical sensation at all. They merely long for a Pepsi-Cola model with whom to be seen arriving at or, better still, departing from some fashionable bar.

People are forever objecting to sexual acts between men on the ground that they are sinful or dirty or anatomically harmful, but the real trouble is that they are contrived. In the early stages of an affair between a man and a woman, it can at least be hoped that their union can be taken for granted–that they can merge in it almost by instinct. This can never be the case for two men; before they get into bed, they must have a board meeting. The soul doesn't have a chance.

CHILDREN, SEX, AND INNOCENCE

Q: What do you think about a child sexually threatened by an adult–a "child molester"?

A: When I am told that a grown man was tampering with small boys, I first ask, "What was he doing with them?" The usual response is a nervous giggle, as if that weren't the issue. But it *is* the issue. If he was only fondling them or persuading them to fondle him, that would be one thing. If he was actively indulging in sodomy with someone who was ten or 11, that's quite another–he would certainly produce a terror of sex in the child, for one thing, and the act would cause real physical damage. So this *is* an issue. And most people pretend that it doesn't matter. Boys of 11 are forever "tampering" with one another, and what does it matter that the park keep has tampered with one of them as long as no physical harm is caused? It makes almost no difference.

Q: So it's the *act.*

A: It's the act: Does taking the passive part in the act of sodomy alter your physical structure if it's repeated often enough, and is it deleterious to your physical health?

Q: However, if the boy is a fast-maturing 13 or 14, and is in effect physically a man, would you worry about the emotional effect?

A: Well, you see, I don't really believe in the emotions. People are always trying to pretend that if you are tampered with by some person much older than yourself, your psyche is scarred for life, and I very much doubt this. I think children chiefly get embarrassed. I remember, when I was a child, two girls rushing home and explaining to their mother that they had been looking for chestnuts in the park, and the park keeper said, "Oh! If I find any, I'll keep them for you, and if you come with me now I'll show you where I'll hide them so that you will find them another day." The girls said, "So we went among the bushes with him and when we got there he stuck himself out at us!" That was the phrase. And the mother said, "Well, what did you do? And they said, "We came away. It all seemed very silly to us." You see, that made absolutely no difference to their lives or their attitudes toward sex.

There are of course circumstances which are quite terrifying. When you learn that girls have been taken by men into some cellar which was almost totally dark and kept there day and night until they submitted to something, this is quite a different thing. However, if they were kept without being sexually abused at all, they would have grown up absolutely terrified of strangers–not of sex.

So it depends upon what is done to the child, what is offered to them, how long the sexual persecution may go on, how much force has been used. You needn't worry about the psychological effect of most sexual tampering; it's what happens physically that counts. Because, you see, when you're young you think you're supposed to respond in some way; later you learn you don't *have* to respond to anything at all.

When I was very young I was made to take, I think, the landlady's dog for a walk in the park in London. And as the dog ran around a bit, a man sat on a bench next to me, and asked me if I was in school. I replied that I was. And he asked me, "Are the boys beaten?" I said, "Occasionally." He asked if they were made to take their trousers down when they were beaten and I said no. He asked, "Wouldn't you prefer that they were made to take their trousers down?" And I said, "What does it matter? What's the difference?" He went on at me, saying, "But you *would* really rather that they were made to take their trousers down, to see them when they were bending over," and I knew he wanted me to say yes, so, in a rather feeble voice, I did. When I got home, I actually told my mother this extraordinary story. That will rather show you how little this had to do with sex. What she thought, I've no idea, but I thought that this was some tiresome old man who was edging me into saying I do or do not approve of something about which I had no opinions whatsoever. And I'm sure I wouldn't have felt this if I were absolutely victimized and made to undergo some sex act which was painful or that I happened to find revolting in some way. This is when it really starts to matter, when you have some reaction against it other than the mere idea that it's sex.

I think there is an idea that children are innocent, which is preserved almost at all costs. People sometimes ask me if I like children, and I say I'm indifferent to them. I treat them exactly as if they are grown up. I say I would hate to be left looking after a child because I wouldn't know what to do. I've had no practice. To me it would be like being left with someone's cat. Why is it running around the room? I couldn't talk to it, it couldn't talk to me. Does it look ill? Why is it *writhing?* Does it want food? I'd feel exactly the same with cats, dogs, what have you.

But other people say about children, "I can't help loving them, they're so innocent." I would ask, of what are they innocent? To which many people reply, "Of duplicity." Do you find grown-up people full of duplicity? Most people may say they do, but I suppose I don't find children particularly innocent because I *don't* find grown-ups particularly devious. I'm surprised when I've been holding a long conversation with somebody and realize it was all about something else. And someone says, "Of course, you know, they really asked you that because they wanted to find out this, that, or the other thing." I'm genuinely amazed because mostly I assume people are doing and saying what they seem to be doing and saying. As for the innocence of children, I don't ever remember being "innocent," or particularly surprised or shocked by anything. I remember I was with a small girl when I was about ten or 11, we smoked cigarettes which we found in a cigarette box which belonged to her father, and then she was found out. I asked her, "What did you do?" "I cried," she said. "What else could I do?" Now, this is an extremely sophisticated remark. It shows she was not innocent. She had to think it out, to do it as a ruse. The idea of being innocent, of not being acquainted with the horrors of the world, the horrors of sex, is something which we have to take carefully. I can imagine a terrible circumstance in which someone would vent their sexual appetite on somebody by force in really horrible ways where the child would only comply to save its life. This is of course wrong. But few forms of sexual tampering are in any way that drastic, and I think you have to be very careful before you say it's *all* wrong, and lump together all forms of tampering with other people, whatever ages you're talking about.

Q: Why do you suppose people say that, that it's wrong across the board?

A: Perhaps so as not to have to face it. Physical reality.

Q: So the only thing to be concerned about is whether or not someone is harmed physically?

A: Yes. Life is, in my opinion, entirely physical.

I read an article recently which said that if you gave criminals the right sort of diet you would be able to alter their entire criminal psychology. I would think this is quite possible.

PART THREE

In which Mr. Crisp explains

THE NATURE OF WIT

Wit is the voice of style.

One might almost define an aphorism as an ugly truth gracefully phrased or say that wit is any comment upon the human condition made in a way that is memorable. Brevity is not the soul of wit. Truth is its soul and brevity its body, but since by now all truths are foregone, it can only be the form that we give them that is our individual contribution. Those who sink to mere trading in facts insult their hearers. We can be offered only two kinds of information—what we already know, which is boring, and what we do not, which is humiliating.

The only kind of merriment that the man in the street does not fear at all is a joke—a prefabricated anecdote that follows the question: "Have you heard this one?" He likes this kind of humor because such tales are always about two other people, never about the speaker and the listener. This is precisely what makes them styleless. The stories that come out of a salesman's notebook exist in isolation. They are inorganic and almost incapable of taking on the personality of the speaker. Also, though some of them may provoke laughter, all of them provoke other, similar tales. An evening spent swapping funny stories quickly takes on the horrible boredom of an amateur variety program. Every few minutes the entertainment stops and then starts again. For a social occasion to have something like the quality of a play, its wit must derive from the very nature of the situation at hand—must be provoked by the diversity of personalities involved.

The only thing that justifies the existence of these tales that people hand round like cigarettes is that the best of them embody a general principle of humor which we can study and put to our own use. We already know that what matters is the order in which we place our words, but this is not enough. We must formulate infallible rules about this order so that, if we wish, we can make our simplest utterances funny.

Whenever people ask us to display or preserve a sense of humor, they want us to accept with equanimity some calculated insult. This request is very annoying, but at least it is based on a genuine idea of what humor is. It is detachment. A true humorist is so totally unengaged that he can relax in any situation and evaluate every crisis—even one brought about by his own folly—from at least two (possibly opposed) points of view. This may seem to be a lot to expect of human nature, but in fact, in some people detachment seems to have known no limits. When Mr. Kierkegaard fell half fainting to the floor at the feet of his friends, they tried to lift up his body and carry him to bed. "Oh, leave it," he murmured. "The maid will sweep it up in the morning."

From a standpoint as remote as this it would be possible to regard any incident as a kind of play, and this is what the ideal raconteur does—using, naturally, the dramatist's two chief weapons, suspense and surprise.

We can observe this theory in practice by examining any well-known joke. Let us take the tale of the faith healer and the child. I choose this one not because it is the funniest story in the world but because its form is classic.

A child goes to a faith healer and says, "Please, sir, Father's ill." The old man explains that these words contain the very root of the patient's malady. "What you mean," he says, "is that your father *thinks* he's ill. Go home and tell him this and in a week's time come back and report on the change in his condition that you will undoubtedly observe." So the child departs, does as he is told, and returns on the appointed day. "Please, sir," he says, "Father thinks he's dead."

Here, almost naked, are the principles on which humor works. First, the words are arranged in such an order that the one containing the surprise is at the end; second, the tragic statement in the second half of the tale is made in optimistic phraseology set up in the first half. This is all there is to it. I deny utterly that the humor of the story depends upon making fun of the doctrines of faith healing. The laughter lodges innocently in the space between form and content.

The work of humorists grows harder with every passing year. There was a time when every large subject had its own built-in quality. Death was solemn; sex was naughty; virtue was sacred. The iconoclasm of our age has altered all this. If we look at the work of humorous authors who were writing before the First World War, we notice this at once. Readers of the short stories of Saki experienced a delicious sense of outrage at the flippancy of Mr. Clovis Sangrail almost every time he opened his mouth.

"When I was young," said Clovis, "my mother taught me the difference between good and evil—only I've forgotten it."

"You've forgotten the difference between good and evil?" gasped the princess.

"Well, she taught me three ways of cooking lobster. You can't remember everything."

Nowadays, when moral distinctions have been erased from the mind not only of Mr. Sangrail but of a whole generation, no one coming across the passage I have quoted (possibly inaccurately) would know at what he was being asked to laugh.

A modern humorist has to impose the required emotional quality on his subject matter by his choice of words and tone of voice before he can start to debunk it. While beginning to tell his story in one mood, he must, like a good thriller writer, foresee the contrary ending.

PART FOUR

In which Mr. Crisp explains

ART

Surrealism was the last artistic movement to draw any concerted response from the British public. The word "surrealism" passed instantly, like vaccine, into our bloodstream and can never be dislodged. Mr. Salvador Dali is not generally considered to be surrealism's greatest artist, but he has certainly been its busiest public relations officer. His antics were in all the papers; his photographs, with his toasting-fork mustache, were in all the magazines; and in case any corner of his personality should remain unlit by the spotlight of publicity, he wrote the story of his life, in which almost everything that other people would regard as frightening or disgusting was described as beautiful. Mr. Dali could be seen to be working very hard at his image. This caused him to be accused of "showing off." Rightly he ignored this. No stylist should ever be afraid of this line of criticism. Without an element of vulgarity, no man can become a work of art.

We must not wonder too greatly at manifestations of childish inconsistency in artists. The visual arts are a regression. Naturally children express themselves in this way; they see such a long time before they speak. But speech, once mastered, is a means of communication so subtle and, more important, so social that to continue to use any other is per-verse. To insist in adult life on smearing surfaces with pig-ment or—an even deadlier giveaway—plunging one's hands into soft clay can only be regarded as infantilism.

If any of the making professions comes under the heading of art, the sticky cliché with which the cracks in it are pasted over is "the joy of creation." In art as in life, there may be a few moments of ecstasy in the act of conception (don't count on this), but bringing anything to birth is usually a long, painful, and appallingly styleless process. Moreover, it takes you away from people.

Q: Would you call yourself an artist?

A: I suppose not really. I have to try and think what an artist is, apart from a hooligan who cannot live within his in-come of praise. I think that unifies all artists. Obviously they are people for whom it is not enough for the girl next door to tell them that they're wonderful. They have to have thou-sands of people say they're wonderful, and failing all else, to say that their *work* is wonderful.

I wouldn't say I was an artist. I think I would partake of the feeling that writing is my vocation. I'm not one of those writers you'll hear say, "When you are a writer, you never retire, you go on writing–that's your life." Living is my life. I write in order to stay alive. I've tried to write as well as I can, but I do feel that the weakness of my writing is that I do always write in the same way. I think very great writers write in one way for *The New York Times,* in another way for *The New Yorker,* and in another way for a novel, but they're able to adapt themselves in the same way that an actress does not appear in a Gilbert and Sullivan opera as she does in a play by Mr. O'Neill. I don't feel I know how to do that. I can only write the way I speak and speak the way I write, which I think is a limitation in my craft. But I wouldn't say I was an artist.

Artists seem to be marked by having a reverence for something which is to me a craft. They live for their own work and regard it as sacred. They care whether it is altered by editors. Whereas I'm absolutely, altogether indifferent. If, once I've written something and an editor says he's got to change it, say it the other way round, I say fine. I want them to be happy. Artists must do things their own way–they feel they are right and that they have the right to be right, but I don't feel any of this. For me, writing is a way first of all to stay alive and then of bringing myself to the notice of the world. It is the world I care about, not the writing.

I do write to reach as many people as possible. It's a desire, I suppose, to spread yourself over the largest available territory. It's a way of owning the world, a way of owning people. The instinct of birds to sing is not, apparently, in the hope of attracting mates; it's the desire to establish territory. I want the widest territory possible–it is a great need.

But if somebody said: This is the end, we're never going to

publish another thing you write, but here's some money you can live on forever, I wouldn't think: Oh! This is terrible—it's like I'm *dead*. It wouldn't worry me in the least.

PART FIVE

In which Mr. Crisp explains

WRITERS & BOOKS

The writing of books can become a very bad habit, but to write one is salutary. Everyone should keep a diary not only of events but also of opinions, ideas, dreams—a record of the soul. In Mr. Dali's book there is a section called "Childhood Memories." It contains some lurid, even hair-raising incidents. The reader becomes calmer when he arrives at the next chapter. This is headed "True Childhood Memories."

A diary is useful not only because it could form the basis for an autobiography but also because it helps to clarify thought, brings to light what the writer's character is like, and gives him some idea of how it will seem to others. In this way it becomes a preparation for living out in the open.

MR. OSCAR WILDE

"I have put my talent into writing," said Mr. Wilde. "My genius I have saved for living."

These words should be woven into samplers and hung above the beds of all would-be stylists. The values seem so right. It is a pity that Mr. Wilde's subsequent actions belied his words.

At first glance Mr. Wilde seemed to have a cast-iron lifestyle—almost to have invented the idea. His appearance was against him. Everything else, however, was in his favor. He had had an education in the arts; he had enough leisure to cultivate his tastes; he had talent, and he had fame. In the days when the music halls were still open, a good test of fame was whether a comedian could raise a laugh by mentioning your name. This test Mr. Wilde passed at "A" level. In *Patience* we have a whole opera the humor of which was originally heightened by recognizing that it was Mr. Wilde who was being lampooned. Even at a time when dandyism was a fashion, he was a conspicuous aesthete who walked down Picadilly with a poppy or a lily in his medieval hand.

Everyone seemed to condone this posture. Because he had as yet done nothing to weaken the structure of their society, audiences laughed at his jokes even though they were about the delights of sin and the boredom of virtue. People found them just shocking enough to be delicious.

Mr. Wilde took his popularity at its face value even though he knew his life could not be judged so superficially. He really seems to have thought that he could rise above common morality while almost certainly knowing that he was already in danger.

When I was young and used to waltz round London's West End, the name of Mr. Wilde was on the lips of every male and female prostitute. He was the subject of innumerable dirty jokes, of diatribes of vilification, and of emotional speeches about sexual freedom. Whatever the moral attitude adopted, the legend on which it was founded was always the same. Mr. Wilde had met a gilded youth called Lord Alfred Douglas, fallen in love with him, and thrown the world away. I believed every word of this.

Now, nearly 50 long, dark years later, when I have known so many homosexuals who could not be prevented from telling me the stories of their lives, I think differently. Strange tales have I heard, but none describing a conversion to homosexuality of Pauline suddenness. From this I conclude that Mr. Wilde had been at least bisexual for a long time before he met Lord Alfred Douglas.

Even the movies about Mr. Wilde did not try to drag any love into the relationship between him and Lord Alfred, although love is a religion to the film industry. They made it clear that the younger man procured youths for the older and then nagged him for money, stopping short of blackmail only because it wasn't practical. He would have been dragged down with his victim.

There is, of course, nothing wrong with being sordid—it makes a rattling good life-style; but Mr. Wilde floundered between sordidness and an almost fatuous conception of beauty. He festooned the dung heap on which he had placed himself with sonnets as people grow honeysuckle around outdoor privies.

His life-style was already weakening. When he sued the Marquis of Queensberry he withdrew it altogether, as sharply as a chameleon retracts its tongue. He should have known that he could not suddenly invoke the laws of a society that he had so volubly professed to despise. Who did he think would come to his aid? When you make fun of people, they laugh not because they feel free of your mockery but because they feel helpless. When they are no longer at your mercy, the laughter dies on their foaming lips.

Within the terms of his life-style Mr. Wilde need never have brought any legal action. He could have feigned to be above confession and denial. Of his friends, some would have known he was queer; some would not—would have been impossible to convince. All implored him to go abroad for a time. Mr. Wilde took no one's advice. He stayed because he was a spiteful man and also because he couldn't bear to leave the stage. This was commendable, but if you are going to hog the limelight you must know exactly which of your acts you are going into. Mr. Wilde did not. When he came to court he tried everything by turns. Asked if he had kissed one of the young men mentioned by the prosecution, he said he had not because the boy was not pretty enough. I would call this remark pert rather than witty. It would only just have got into one of his plays. Later in the same trial he had the nerve to cite poor Mr. Plato, who died a philosopher and came back as a spinster's alibi. He also launched himself into a long speech holding up the "love that dares not speak its name" as a love that is pure. For all I know, such love may exist, but the time to go on about it is not when there has been read out in court a list as long as your arm of boys you never met except in heavily curtained rooms in Oxford.

From the verdict onward, Mr. Wilde seems to have fallen apart still further. In jail he attempted a complete reversal of style, which can be very effective, but it is an unalterable law that the new image must be brighter than the one that has been abandoned. Here this was not the case. The verses that he wrote before his imprisonment could not be described as anything more than pretty, but "The Ballad of Reading Gaol" contains almost every hitherto foregone epithet imaginable.

I have known personally men who have served sentences twice as long as Mr. Wilde's and who immediately afterward have taken up their lives again, neither refusing to mention nor insisting on dilating upon their experience. Why did Mr. Wilde emerge from prison a broken man?

As I see it, it was his style that was broken. It was never a part of him but rather it was a sequined Band-Aid covering a suppurating sore of self-hatred.

MISS GERTRUDE STEIN

Miss Gertrude Stein was greater than Mr. Wilde in that she used a small—some said a nonexistent—gift as a colorless fluid in which to suspend a monstrous ego.

It is heartening, when comparing these two so very different writers, to be able to point out that though both of them sought worldwide admiration, neither was beautiful in a universally acceptable way. Mr. Wilde's appearance was such that on first seeing him, Lord Alfred Douglas was sorry for him, while Miss Stein, whether in photographs or in Mr. Picasso's portrait of her (painted in her absence), looked like an obstinate middle-aged man.

Though Miss Stein had no beauty, she did have other things. One of these was enough money to indulge her whims. In accordance with the laws of style, she did not allow these to multiply. By the time the world began to hear of her, she had only two. The first concerned her environment.

She wished to live where culture grows wild. She therefore

left America for Europe. "Art in this century," she said, "is something done by Spaniards in France." Once across the Atlantic, she set about picking artists in handfuls. This she managed by the simple and practical expedient of buying their pictures. Having made the acquaintance of Mr. Picasso, Mr. Picabia, and others, she cemented her relationship with them by inviting them to dinner and arranging the table so that each painter sat opposite one of his pictures. All this demonstrates her singleness of purpose and her cunning, but she must also have possessed some other quality. It is well known that the only solid food taken by artists is the flesh of patronesses' hands, which distasteful fare they wash down with swigs of absinthe. Yet no one ever seems to have despised Miss Stein. Those who were not members of her immediate circle wished they were. Almost every American of that era who had any artistic pretensions whatever ran all the way to her house the moment his boots struck the beaches of Normandy.

Miss Stein's second whim concerned herself. She was not content to carry a banner in the great cultural protest march of her decade; she wanted to wield her own pitchfork or ax or scythe at the storming of the establishment. It was not enough to rule her own coterie; she wanted, like Yum-Yum, to rule the earth.

All around her the visual arts were being convulsed by cubism, futurism, and other forms of abstraction. Miss Stein decided to perform a parallel act of liberation for literature.

Her crusade was doomed. Color and, to a lesser extent, shape—especially on a huge scale—evoke a certain emotional response whether they represent recognizable objects or not.

Words have almost no power outside their meanings. Alliteration, onomatopoeia, assonance, and all the other Tennysonian tricks work only in alignment with the sense of the phrase they decorate. If they move in a contrary direction they become inert.

Miss Stein disregarded these eternal laws completely and, to provoke her readers further, did not call her writings verse. Had she done this, like Mr. e.e. cummings, she might somewhere have won a little dazed acceptance. Miss Elizabeth Barrett's maid was not the only person who did not expect to understand poetry. Some would rather die. Ignoring this loophole, Miss Stein referred to her shorter pieces as stories, though they had no narrative content whatsoever. Even to say this gives to the uninitiated no hint of the anarchy that rages therein. One of these items ends thus: "Stew stew than."

Miss Stein also penned portraits of people whom she knew, but here again, in none of these did there arise any image of the person whose name was superscribed. As an illustration I quote the beginning of "The Portrait of Constance Fletcher": "O the bells that are the same are not stirring and the languid grace is not out of place and older fur is disappearing...."

In this style Miss Stein wrote a great deal. She had to in order to convince the world that even if she was mad, she was sincere. In this she ultimately succeeded. That her work was printed is not surprising. She paid. After a while she did better than this. Her sheer persistence–that massive belief in oneself that is one of the prerequisites of style–bludgeoned some publishers into taking her seriously. When she was sufficiently famous for *Harper's Bazaar* to print a parody of her prose, she wrote at once to the editor and asked why the magazine did not publish the real thing. "It's much funnier," she pointed out. The contribution she sent appeared in a subsequent issue. From this tiny incident we see that she was prepared not merely to accept but to invite ridicule, while never openly admitting that she wrote as she did for laughs. In this she resembled those actresses who, playing in melodrama, if they fail to make their audience weep, overact until they provoke laughter. There is a vertiginous tightrope stretched between pomposity and clowning that all stylists must be prepared to walk.

When asked why she wrote at all, Miss Stein spread out her arms and cried, "For praise; for praise; for praise."

It's a wonder she didn't starve. She would have if she had not been ready to accept, instead of adoration, a few crumbs of blame. Yet she would not gobble up any old crusts of publicity. Along with all other stylists, in the midst of excess she drew the line somewhere. She lived in France–that country to which lesbianism is what cricket is to England–yet, though she looked like a man and lived for a lifetime in domestic simplicity with Miss Alice Toklas, she seems seldom to have spoken and never to have written about her love life. She wanted literary notoriety or none.

Nothing remains of her empire. Of all her books, the most readable is *Everybody's Autobiography*. This is doubtless still on the shelves of many public libraries, but I should be surprised if it is often borrowed. A few years ago, in an effort to revive her memory, someone wrote a biography of her called *The Third Rose*. It seemed to cause little stir. The difficulty of recreating the quality of a stylist is almost insurmountable.

Stylists are not interesting for what they write or for what they do but for something that they are.

Not only without looks but without much talent or even sense, Miss Stein, by sheer force of personality, got to know everyone she wanted to know and became a household word throughout the American-speaking world.

MR. ERNEST HEMINGWAY

Among the many Americans who visited the court of Miss Stein was Mr. Ernest Hemingway. On one occasion he held a very significant conversation with her. It was about homosexuality. Miss Stein defended its practice among women–as well she might–and explained that female homosexuality was less perverse and cleaner than homosexuality among men. She evidently thought that all physical relations between males were sodomitic. Mr. Hemingway did not argue this point but condemned all sexual deviation. His views on the subject were so strong that he said a man must be prepared to kill rather than submit. Usually, when an overture of this nature is made to a grown man, his slightest frown is sufficient to cause the other party to go and join the Foreign Legion. It is therefore difficult to imagine where, outside the novels of Mr. David Storey, the rape of one man by another is a likelihood.

Mr. Hemingway's remark sounds less like an expression of considered moral condemnation than an almost involuntary cry uttered in some obsessive, lurid dream. This perpetual nightmare was what provoked and maintained the author's life-style.

Though not exactly autobiographical, his novels were adventure stories whose heroes were nearly always excessively masculine men of action, and as Mr. Hemingway grew older, so did they. Unlike Mr. Kipling and Mr. Galsworthy, two other writers who liked the idea of a man's world, he did not seem to think of women as a nuisance or as a means of acquiring property. He described his heroines with affection but not with great understanding. To have identified himself with them even for the purpose of literature might have brought back the terrible dream of androgyny. He may even have feared that there was something effete about the occupation of writing fiction of any kind. To atone for this he displayed in his life a degree of courage that came near to making it a parody of his books. He fought in all the available wars, fell out of airplanes, and shot everything that moved throughout the length and breadth of Africa. In the end he even shot himself. People always refer to this last act as "the final tragedy." I cannot imagine why. In a way, all death, and because of it, all life, is tragic. About life the hero of *A Farewell to Arms* says, "It kills the very good and the very gentle and the very brave impartially. If you are none of these you can be sure it will kill you in the end but there will be no special hurry." Surely it is only in this general sense that Mr. Hemingway's death is tragic.

A man may keep on writing far into the night of senility—many authors do—but if he is a man of action he cannot, in the fullest sense, continue to live those last years. To me, Mr. Hemingway's suicide represents a triumph of style over life. It shows that he regarded his existence as a work of art requiring a definite outline. His action puts Mr.

Wilde, for all his protestations, to shame.

Unlike Miss Stein, Mr. Hemingway did not have to perform the feat of balancing his prodigious personality on a slender literary gift. He wrote a great deal and, right from the beginning, his work was almost universally admired. His problem was therefore the opposite of hers—how to stomp about in the flow of his fiction without drowning. He succeeded.

Except for a sense of humor, Mr. Hemingway had everything. He was as handsome as the sun; his constitution seemed almost indestructible; he had talent; he had fame; and after movies had been made of *A Farewell to Arms,* "The Snows of Kilimanjaro," "The Killers," and "The Short Happy Life of Francis Macomber," he was rich. What is more, he made the fullest use of every one of these attributes. Of all the writers whom I can call to mind, he is the one whose lifestyle not only was in keeping with what he wrote but transcended it.

MR. NORMAN MAILER

Mr. Mailer is just as rugged as Mr. Hemingway but more modern. Because morality has changed, he has constituted himself not a hero but an antihero; he has become less a man of action than a symbol of social subversion. Mr. Hemingway championed the underdog. In the war in Spain he was on the losing side, but we must never say that he fought for communism because he knew it could not win.

It is Mr. Mailer who espouses lost causes. While Mr. Hemingway may have been the victim of neurotic self-assurance,

Mr. Mailer is the exponent of boisterous self-doubt. He seems to embrace failure and has compelled the world press to snap him in this compromising position.

His marriages are solemnized like wrongs hushed up, but his divorces are reported in as much detail as a boxing match; if he ever rejoices he must do so in a whisper, but his curses are on a coast-to-coast network. If he were to receive an award we should never know about it, but when he is clapped into a dungeon the police can hardly reach him through the convoy of cameramen. Since it is at his special request that the photographers are present, we must say that disgrace is part of his style. Defeat is the medium through which he fully intends to reach out and touch his audience.

After the success of *The Naked and the Dead,* Mr. Mailer need never have got out of bed again. If he did so it must be because he did not feel that he had yet entered the profession of being. With *Why Are We in Vietnam?* and *The Armies of the Night* he moved forward from the writing of novels to the more direct profession of pamphleteering. All his later work, however entitled, is really the bulkiest letter ever delivered to the President–any president. The only blemish on this mammoth gesture is the rejection in his writing of the word "I." Many writers have used the fictional first person; Mr. Mailer has invented the autobiographical third. It is an ingenious device but seems a little coy in so bold a man.

Needless to say, the mere writing of pamphlets soon ceased to be enough for Mr. Mailer; he now acts them out. In this way style has been brought to protest. To crystallize his rebellion, he has produced, directed, and acted in a movie called *Wild 90.* In real life something might go wrong–or what other people would call right. A policeman might for once be merciful to one of his victims. But in a film of his own devising Mr. Mailer is certain of suffering in person and forever the desired injustice. He fixes eternally before our eyes the blackened image of authority against which he shines so brightly.

Mr. Fred Astaire once said to Mr. Jack Lemmon, "You're at a level where you can only afford one mistake. The higher up you go, the more mistakes you're allowed. Right at the top, if you make enough of them, it's considered to be your style."

He must have been thinking of Mr. Mailer.

M. JEAN GENET

Degradation is the style embraced by M. Jean Genet. He committed so many crimes that finally he was condemned to life imprisonment. The sentence was never carried out because M. Jean Cocteau successfully petitioned the French government for a pardon. Thus was justice tempered with artistic snobbery—almost with idiocy.

If a man's crime is theft, the only extenuating circumstance that can be adduced is overwhelming need. This was never discussed. Instead it was pointed out that M. Genet was a genius. As this is another way of saying that it would have been comparatively easy for him to earn a living in a different way, this argument ought logically not to have secured his release but rather to have aggravated his punishment. What an opportunity was waiting there for a display of official style! The judge might have said, "The court was not previously aware of the prisoner's many accomplishments. In view of these, we see fit to impose the death penalty."

His pardon was granted in accordance with the erroneous but almost universally held idea that culture belongs to France and that for a Frenchman to exhibit talent is a kind of patriotism. M. Cocteau is now dead. We can never know but only hope that he was shamelessly exploiting the chauvinism of his own countrymen in order to ameliorate the lot of a man who was, in some respects, a kindred spirit. If, on the contrary, he sincerely subscribed to the notion that there is a close connection between aesthetic and moral values, it is a great pity. This kind of confused thinking (which we also see in operation when books are exempted from censorship on the ground that they are well-written) leads to words like "good," "moral," "true," "beautiful" all acquiring the same meaning.

Forgiven by M. Cocteau, M. Genet was then canonized by M. Jean-Paul Sartre, who called him the saint of existentialism, and, in a way, he is. If existentialism is the philosophy that decrees that you can only exercise your free will by swimming with the tide but faster, then it is the creed of style, and M. Genet is certainly a stylist. Fate bestowed upon him certain special advantages. He was illegitimate and spent his childhood in an orphanage. From there he graduated to a reformatory. If at this point he had not believed in the importance of a life-style, he might have tried to throw off the burdens of his early years, to turn again and become mayor of Paris. He wisely saw that this would be to yield his unique advantage and lose momentum on his journey toward self-realization. Having started downhill, he soon broke into a run toward his chosen goal of degradation. Though his homosexuality seems a thousand times more natural than Mr. Wilde's, part of its appeal does appear to be the opportunity it gives him to heap social opprobrium upon himself.

M. Sartre says that M. Genet knows that he will never commit murder. If this is true, it is to be regretted. The act that would crown M. Genet's life would be to kill someone—ideally M. Sartre—by sexual assault.

Compared with the life that M. Genet has led, writing must seem a very tame occupation, but in spite of this he has found time to write three plays and several books. One of these, *Our Lady of the Flowers,* is described by the author as a prolonged fantasy with which he whiled away the hours while he was in prison. This is explanation enough. While he could not fully live, he wrote. Another of his works is called *The Thief's Journal.* This book is said to be autobiographical, but the reader cannot help feeling that here also we have a large element of daydream. It seems so unlikely that the author, picking his way with whatever care, would never have met anyone of normal sexual dimensions.

In M. Genet's life, the fantasy, the fiction, the reality are mixed with a marvelous degree of homogenization. No one can separate the various elements in his life-style. He is famous because he has written books that have been widely read, and his work is widely read because the public knows that he has lived it.

This situation has been made possible by the moral laxity at present fashionable. The '40s and '50s were the age of recorded suffering. In accordance with that divine law by which everything always gets worse, the '60s and '70s were

the age of recorded depravity. At one time few people read
books of a documentary nature. They preferred fiction. They
felt sure it would contain descriptions of goings-on that decorum and fear of the laws of libel would automatically ex-
punge from works founded on fact. The odds are now reversed: Biographies and autobiographies contain material as
salacious as can be found in any novel.

MR. GEORGE BERNARD SHAW
(AND W. B. YEATS)

George Bernard Shaw was an Irishman and George
Bernard Shaw was red-haired and till the end of his life, I believe, he had a slight Irish accent. He had the Irish tempera-
ment in that he was showy but the opposite of the Irish tem-
perament in that he was extremely abstemious. This hatred
of physical life is, I think, not an Irish characteristic. He was
a Puritan without bringing morality into it. He was a true
vegetarian, and I think he found the idea of eating meat disgusting. I don't think he cared about the poor little sheep, and
the poor little goats, and the poor little cows—I think he found
the eating of meat nasty without sentimentalizing it. In most
things he found physical life nasty. This was one of the large
characteristics of his life. He spent more time dealing with
reason, with the mind, with cerebral motives, than with pas-
sions. His plays are very seldom about passion. His plays are
mostly about reason as a truer force.

He had genuine wit. He said things which were a crystal-
lization of certain aspects of the human condition, if we op-

pose him to people like Noël Coward, who mistook bitchiness for wit, and who hardly ever said anything you can now quote as being a comment on life, love, the sky, the sea, whatever. (When Shaw said it is easier to run a democracy if you have a monarch, this is a wonderful high truth.) There is almost no bitchiness in Shaw. Hardly ever is there a reference to anyone's appearance.

Most of Shaw's plays deal with moral dilemmas such as whether the Salvation Army should ask for money from a munitions plant. They're genuine moral dilemmas. He thought of himself as a rebel. When he began he was, I believe, the music critic for a certain paper. As I've no knowledge of music, I don't know whether he was a good music critic or a bad one. He was probably a witty one; that is to say, he could describe a certain kind of music in a way which would make you say, "Oh, I wish I'd said that." Then he became a dramatic critic, and his plays got more and more profound. You get to *Saint Joan,* which I think we must regard as the greatest play in the English language in modern times. *Saint Joan* is very long, very wordy, but it does have remarkable dramatic effects, though I think Shaw probably regarded himself as avoiding dramatic effects. Nevertheless, when the whole of the Inquisitor's speech has been made somebody says, "Now will you sign this recantation?" and Saint Joan replies, "I cannot write. But I can make my mark." That is an *incredible* dramatic effect. And this he was capable of, although he was always, I think, trying to avoid it. I think he wished not at any cost to be seen to be aiming at dramatic effect.

Q: How would you compare Shaw and Wilde?

A: Shaw and Wilde, who were both Irish, wished to be personalities in the perfectly ordinary sense of the word–they wished to appear in the press. Shaw adopted the attitude that he had no idea what was being said about him, but this is absolute nonsense.

He lived to a great old age. He went on writing plays, which, of course, inevitably got weaker and weaker. They're innocent and too good to be true. Even *The Apple Cart* is weak, though it's very funny. And in the end, as you know, he said to the nurse, "You are needlessly prolonging my life." He is a testament to this life of austerity in which you eat no meat, and don't eat much of anything else, and have no sex life. The theory is that he had sexual relations with Mrs. Shaw before marriage but never afterward. I think we must say he was an extremely abstemious person. He had a thin, bony frame and adored being seen in a scanty swimsuit in middle age in the South of France. There's no doubt he sought publicity; he liked it, he provoked the press.

He was a much more solid, aware, coordinated, consistent person than Mr. Wilde, who was a troubled soul, totally incapable of seeing himself as the world saw him. Shaw was very realistic. He did of course have these mad *theories,* about spelling, for example. He wanted all to be phonetic. But this I think was a sort of joke. I don't think he thought it would ever happen.

He had answers ready. When he came to America and they asked him something to do with the American Constitution, he said, "Don't ask me. I've been here before. I've told you what to do and you haven't done it."

Q: That sounds like you, sometimes. I've heard you say, "Well, I tell people how to be happy but they don't listen!"

A: Yes. He said that too.

I think Shaw was convinced of his own ideas. I think he *did* think, for example, that if spelling were all to be reduced to phonetics it would all be much easier. I would say he had some reason for all of his thoughts, but did he care? No, I don't think he would have founded a society where alternate spelling was the rule, made himself the president of it, or done any of these things. He seems to have been able to court the world and remain aloof from it at the same time. He had the oddest friends–Lawrence of Arabia was one. I suppose that there was a certain Irishness in the wish to wake up the English and say things to provoke them.

He thought he was better than Shakespeare. He claimed that the only play he could not improve upon was *King Lear,* but this of course left out the poetry of Shakespeare. Shaw despised poetry. But if you compare him to Yeats, the greatest Irish poet, Yeats is mystical, semireligious, poetic, dark, glorious...the great poet of Ireland. He wrote about Irish things, he wrote about fairyland. Now, an English poet would be ashamed to write about fairyland, but he was not in the least ashamed. He wrote with more passion–more self-evident passion–than English writers do. Sorrow is the very atmosphere of Ireland, and this Yeats was to encompass.

When the countess Kathleen is dead, the angel explained

to her, she will be forgiven, she will be taken into heaven—and then the nurse says: "Tell them that we will walk upon the floor of peace that I would die and go to her I love. The years like great black oxen tread the world, and God the herdsman goads them on behind, and I am broken by their oxen feet."

This is Irish poetry, not English poetry.

Shaw despised all that, but I think it's impossible not to admire him. When he lived, people were always saying what a monstrous show-off he was, and why, at his age, with his education, was he always frisking about making a fool of himself? That was the attitude of the English toward Shaw. But I don't think it's possible not to take him seriously. If there were a graph of English drama, its last high point would end with Shaw, and then there would be a slight comedown by the time we got to Osborne.

MR. D. H. LAWRENCE

I did read a great deal of D. H. Lawrence, including the poetry. The poetry is sometimes wonderful and sometimes merely a sort of lay expressionism. To me the great work of Lawrence is the short stories. The novels are stretched out and repetitive, not only of themselves but of one another. And he got away with—before you've gotten to page 150 in almost any of his books—"She trembled before his dark beauty." And then, well, you think: Oh, *that* again. But certainly *Sons and Lovers,* which was before he'd gotten round to sex, is a wonderful book, and I should think it's largely autobiographical—

it concerns his relationship with his mother, which is very profound. The other wonderful book, which to my mind crystallizes the whole of this mystical rubbish about sex, is *The Plumed Serpent.* Very long, but it is very, very wonderful. But the great things are the short stories. He had to confine himself. There are at least a dozen good short stories, of which the greatest is "The Woman Who Rode Away." It is the essence of Lawrence, this desire to find an all-embracing religion which will unify the whole of things. There was the idea that it could all be unified if only we could think of it in the right way.

As a rule, I would not dream of dragging an author's life into a criticism of his work. I think this is very tiresome. But with D. H. Lawrence, it's irresistible. There is a postcard showing him standing beside Frieda Lawrence. There is this ill, consumptive, pointed, bearded man, and beside him is this monolith of a woman. And the moment you see them you know that he never got her to do a single thing he wanted her to do. His books contain Gudrun, who wanted to have her own way, and Ursula, who was acquiescent. Then there's Kate in *The Plumed Serpent,* who wanted to live her own life, and then the wife of Cipriano, who expected nothing and said at one moment, "Where all is given there can be no betrayal." In other words, if you've given your life over utterly to somebody, you can't press him about what he does with it. This is, I think, D. H. Lawrence's ideal, that there must somewhere be this woman whose life warrants the giving of herself utterly to a man. This is what he missed in his own life.

Q: Was Lawrence homosexual?

A: We have to be very careful because homosexuals are the great missionaries of the world and they must not be allowed to say that, really, everybody is homosexual. But it is very noticeable, except in *Lady Chatterley,* where there is a description of the heroine's beauty and the effect it has on the hero, how much time he spent describing the men. The gamekeeper in *The White Peacock* is described including the fact that "his arm entirely filled his sleeve." I can't think of anybody who had the same faintly perverse interest in masculinity.

Q: And the wrestling scene in *Women in Love?*

A: Well, that now of course has been brought to our horrified attention by the movie, which was the first glimpse of you-know-what on the English screen. And yes, it is all a part of his worship. Whether it's directly sexual or not isn't the point. There is this worship of the idea of the physical man, this great, powerful, and overpowering being, born to rule Creation, which is more noticeable, I think, in D. H. Lawrence—because his work is so palpitating and so physical—than in anyone else. There are other people, like Kipling, who quite obviously regarded women as a nuisance—but there's never anywhere else this almost verbal *caressing* of the idea of a man. There is an absolutely fatuous conversation in *Lady Chatterley* between Lady Chatterley's father and the gamekeeper, which is in part about his sexual organ, so unlikely as to be ludicrous, but nevertheless it is there in the book. It's as though Mr. Lawrence either had or wished he had conversations with men about their sexual processes. Even if he never had an affair with a man, which would make him technically homosexual, he had this strange worship of manhood.

MR. ANDY WARHOL*

Did you for one moment imagine that all you had to do was to paint a tin of soup 81 times life-size and straightaway you would rule the world and be costarred in a movie with Mrs. Burton?

Not a chance! You have to have a totally original mind in a totally original body. I know that now because I've read *From A to B & Back Again.* Unfortunately, Mr. Warhol's amazing progress from the obscurity of a Czech ghetto to cosmic renown is not traced in logical detail. The book is only autobiographical by default. Incidents in his life or phases of it are described merely to furnish proof of the rightness of his opinions about art, sex, beauty, or fame. On this last subject he says, "You shouldn't get stuck thinking your product is you, your fame, your aura."

You could've fooled me.

In spite of this undeniable sketchiness, the book is completely naked. I do not use this word in its Paul Morrissey sense. You can strike from your hearts all memory of those boring movies. Though the book is shameless, it is not shocking by modern standards—or, rather, the lack of them. It is truthful—even, at times, defenseless.

What makes Mr. Warhol so unusual is his preoccupation with things. His writings contain whole pages about underwear. Perhaps this is the first ever glimpse into the soul of a visual artist. I, who am none, was once astonished at being asked by a shop assistant what color I would like my toilet roll to be. Mr. Warhol would have taken his purchase back to the shop if, when unwrapped at home, it had turned out not to be just the right shade.

The mere object to which the author pays most attention of all is his body–pimply, pale, thin. "After makeup," he says, "clothes make the man." Is this possibly the key to this great mystery–the weirdest since the *Marie Celeste,* which in some ways his life resembles–miraculously afloat but totally unmanned? Did he simply *have* to be great to compensate him for the so keenly felt poverty of his looks? It is hard to say, because his ideal of beauty is a Schraffts restaurant.

This book is as perceptive as the work of Miss Stein ("Buying is more American than thinking") but is free of her fatuous highbrowism; it is as witty as Miss Dorothy Parker ("Being born is like being kidnapped"), but because it is more outlandish, it seems less embittered; it is as funny as *Gentlemen Prefer Blondes* but not so condescending, because Mr. Warhol *is* Lorelei.

Though he worships the '60s, it is of the '20s that his work constantly reminds us. He knew so many girls with names like Taxi who were rich beyond the wildest dreams of Inland Revenue but, in spite of this, kept shops (unsuccessfully, of course) and died young.

In its flavor the writing of Mr. Warhol is like that of Mr. Evelyn Waugh. As literature there is no comparison. Every word written by the Englishman was meticulously considered; the American appears to have planned nothing–except to plan nothing. When he gives instructions, he always hopes they will be misunderstood. Because of this reverence for the unexpected, in his book the garlic is mixed with the sapphires; platitudes lie next to gems of wisdom.

Mr. Warhol never reads reviews of himself, so I can tell you quietly that his book is quirky above and beyond the call of fashion. Not only the title but even the title pages are contrived and, throughout, the grammar is appalling, but these defects make no serious difference. *From A to B* is a book you simply have to read. Nay, I have not said enough. It is a book you must learn by heart.

* *Review of The Philosophy of Andy Warhol: From A to B and Back Again.*

PART SIX

In which Mr. Crisp explains

THE MOVIES

When we turn our eyes toward the movies, our pulses quicken; the shadows on the landscape grow sharper; the background music swells. By these and other traditional signs we are made aware that we are approaching the spot where the treasure lies buried. We have entered the region where once the sacred mushroom of personality grew as tall as the sequoias.

The movies have been through many phases. In the beginning, quite naturally, audiences felt only amazement that such an invention existed. It was not until Mr. Cecil B. De-Mille arrived in California that people stopped merely staring at the pictures and started looking through the screen aperture into a world of dreams. Even then it was the story that mattered most. However basic it was, because it was being told in an unfamiliar medium it was difficult to follow and demanded total attention. I myself did not begin going to the pictures for about ten years after this phase began. By then, in the early '20s, stars such as Miss Pauline Frederick were already claiming more public notice than the narrative. Mr. D. W. Griffith wished to prevent this shift of emphasis. The way Miss Lillian Gish, with unconquerable tact, tells it, this seems like a miscalculated public relations job.

As I see it, like a true stylist the creator was doing everything in his power to avoid being eclipsed by his cast. He failed. His public was simply not sophisticated enough to take in the idea of a director's film. This concept was not popularized for another 20 years. Then the fair name of Mr. Alfred Hitchcock began to be printed in the credits of his films as large as those of his leading players. In Mr. Griffith's time people were absolutely unaware of the technical devices that he was inventing at the rate of almost one a day (even the word "film," which is basically a more technical term than the word "picture," was hardly ever used). The camera was the audience's eye, and with it all they wished to do was to gorge themselves upon every aspect of the divine being.

I came from a middle-class family living in Sutton, which is a suburb 12 miles outside London, in Surrey, and because I went to my first movies with my mother it was to some extent with her limited vision that I saw them. (I don't remember my father ever going inside a cinema.) I was in a secret trance while each episode of *The Phantom Rider* lasted, but afterward I pretended to think it ludicrous. One of the great jokes at home was to clasp one's hands and roll one's eyes as actors did on the screen. In my mother's view, the pictures were all right for children and the lower classes, but they were trivial and, worse, they were American. For people of refinement there was only the theater.

I was at least 17 before I was often with people who talked without condescension about the movies. My professor of literature said, "If you want to understand Shakespeare, go to the cinema." Even so, I and most of the rest of his students interpreted him to mean that we were to go to culture films (German) rather than entertainment ones (American).

Thus it was that more than a decade of moviemania had passed me by. I am amazed at this, for it is impossible to exaggerate the influence that the cinema had on urban life during the last phase of the silent movies and the beginning of the era of talkies.

Apparently, from the industry's own point of view, the peak years were 1946 and 1947, but even if more seats were sold during those years, people occupied them less wholly. By then Londoners had all played at least bit parts in their very own Technicolor wide-screen production–the war (though many complained that it was less moving than the silent version released 20 years earlier). They now went to the pictures merely to relax. During the late '20s and early '30s they had gone to worship. That was when so many cathedral-sized cinemas loomed up in Edgware Road that they seemed to stand shoulder to neo-Egyptian shoulder.

In those darkened temples people lived the vivid hours of their lives; the dreary residue endured outside passed like a trance. It is useless to ask which level of experience was the more real. Reality is only the dream in which our enemies believe.

In modern times our imaginations are enthralled by less poetic myths. We believe in statistics. Among other things these tell us that movies are made for a girl between the ages of 15 and 20–preferably with an unhappy love life. This piece of information would not formerly have been of much help. The movie industry operates in the realm of the affections and there, until a few years ago, all women were 15.

The term "a woman's film" is fairly new, not because an opportunity to weep is a recently discovered pleasure but because at one time there was no other kind of movie. Although stars were advertised as having S.A. or It or Oomph, it was never with the hope of luring men into the cinema. The portion of the male population that went to the pictures did so in order to sit with their girls in the dark. The women went, not for a reciprocal fumble, but to gather material for the dream of which these smash-and-grab raids on the part of their menfolk deprived them.

Sex may have already come to real life, but comfortable sex was still a long way off. Proof of this lies in the look of the poorer districts of London at night. They are occupied, if at all, only by people on their way somewhere else. During the dreaming years, there was not a dark doorway between King's Cross and Paddington that did not partly conceal a couple that for politeness's sake we will describe as courting.

Faintly bawdy songs about film stars were well-known, but I never heard a man express any real desire for any of the divine women. The great female stars were worshiped by girls because in their looks, in the tone of their voices, must lie the key to the Pentagon of sex–that stronghold from which all men could be ruled and life (meaning sex) could be enjoyed on a woman's terms.

The films of that era were truly immoral. They were governed by strict–almost ludicrously strict–rules about what areas of human skin could be exposed to the cameras, about how long a kiss on the lips should last, and about how much of a man's body must remain off the bed while he was attempting rape. The stories, where after all immorality must always reside, were subject to far less careful supervision. Almost every vehicle for a female star carried the same message: You can have your sexual cake and eat it. Since these films were shown to total believers at a time when, in fact, virginity before marriage was still all the rage, they were, to say the least, misleading.

Thickly unmade-up, the leading lady would say farewell to her good, kind parents and set off for the wicked city. She had hardly taken her seat in the train before Mr. Lionel Atwill was asking, "What is a first-class girl like you doing a third-class compartment?" From that moment onward it was down, down, down she went while her dressmaker's bills rose higher and higher. After hours of degradation, her soul sick of sin and her skeleton bowed by the sheer weight of fur and precious metal, she took refuge in the arms of any one of the industry's stuffies–Mr. Clive Brook or Mr. Herbert Marshall.

As each new star went through these rituals of fall and redemption, she was packaged by Mr. Louis B. Mayer and his merry men as holding the new, improved stratagem for vanquishing men. Since the movies were not run by scientists but by abominable showmen, every discovery was put forward as the final answer.

The posters were hardly dry on the billboards before a thunderous din like the sound track of *Red River* was heard throughout the island. It was caused by the hooves of thousands of women as they rushed upstairs to their bedrooms to throw out the aids to the now obsolete image and get to work on the new.

In the late '20s the streets of London were entirely overrun with near-Garbos; in the early '30s by failed Dietrichs. Before Miss Veronica Lake was finally drained, thousands of girls had been dragged by their hair into looms, through mangles, and under presses as though they were living in a mechanized Aztec kingdom, merely because this particular actress wore her hair hanging over one eye.

Wherever two or three women were gathered together–in factories, in kitchens, in laundries–from dawn till day's end the conversation consisted of each of them acting out the entire story of the current release to all her workmates–with actions, if there was room.

Of course, the girls in the balcony seats never did learn the secret of style, because, in their haste, they neglected to do their homework. Between visits to movie palaces, they indulged in daylong fantasies instead of submitting themselves to limited periods of grueling self-examination. It is a pity, for they stood at the entrance to the richest mine of style ever opened.

What went wrong? Once again life and art began that fatal movement toward each other. Whenever this occurs, it must not be blamed on the philistines alone. It is often they who would like art to remain pure and free from the compromises of the world, and when they do wish for a convergence of art and life it is usually because they want life to be more stylish. In the case of the movies, in their faltering way the devotees tried to become as beautiful as their idols, and life has abetted them. Wealth, leisure, sex, and false eyelashes have gradually been brought within reach of all. This seems to me a good thing. What is bad is the movement from the other side.

Artists never accept for long the limitations of their medium. They never seem aware that these are what give their art its style.

The decline of art is always from realism to naturalism. Realism is usually a technique of subtraction by which an artist lays bare the essence of his subject; naturalism is always a trick of addition with which a charlatan seeks to give conviction to a lie. In the art of moviemaking this disintegration was a particularly sad story because, in the beginning, so much ground lay between it and real life–literally. Now pictures have even lost their national style and are made wherever money is available, but once they were almost all made in a desert on the other side of the world. In that paradise there were no buildings–only sets; no people–only actors. From the dawn of Miss Pickford to the end of a perfect Miss Doris Day, not one sincere word was spoken. Even when sound came it brought with it an unexpected fringe benefit. At first its use presented such technical difficulties that the whole industry moved indoors. Then not only the cast but every stick and stone surrounding it was artificial.

This happy state of affairs could not last. Talkies moved out into the streets and even began to boast that they were doing so. At the same time, as with stage stars, movie actresses allowed it to be known that they were human. During the reign of Mr. Mayer, truth about players under contract to him came only from his lips. Not only their faces but even their lives were made-up. This kept their life-style all of a piece. Now, even if the human race still had a capacity for wonder, it could not lavish it upon film actresses. We know their real names; we know their real measurements; and when magazines like *Confidential* still flourished, we knew or thought we knew about their bizarre bedroom antics. It is true that even after it became known that Mr. Zeus was a sex maniac he remained a god, but few people have a public relations department like his. The stars lost their glitter, and decadence set in. Audiences then began to take an interest in the movies themselves—not in the stories they told but in the manner of telling them. Instead of rejoicing in the triumph of virtue, they got enthusiastic about accurate postsynchronization and skillful back-projection.

When the movies abandoned the star system they did not lose everything but gave up what was uniquely theirs. No other medium can so fully deploy physical style. No other art form is at once so intimate and so distant. The cinema allowed an audience to spy on its heroine as though from a nearby window with powerful binoculars. The subject appeared not to know she was being watched. She did not pause for laughs or raise her voice above the sound of coughing in the auditorium, as mere stage actresses do. She continued her private life undisturbed, thus giving us the exciting feeling that there was nothing, however personal, that she might not do. Yet we could scrutinize her so closely that we saw her skin texture and watched the beating of her heart. This combination of opposing qualities made every film into an overheard scandal, compared with which a play, performed with semaphore gestures and spoken with tub-thumper's diction, is as intimate as a parade ground command.

We knew the stars as we know God. They were all-pervading but remote; we created them, but their fate was not our fate, and they remained intractable, unlikely to respond to our prayers.

Movies were not made in sequence. The whole purpose of this stratagem was to save money—to make full use of one set before striking it—but unintentionally it conferred on the final product an extra benefit. Actresses could survive this patch-work method of manufacture, could give their performances any degree of consistency, only by perfecting a set of idio-syncrasies. The more predictable these gestures came to be, the more inevitable rightness the character acquired. What audiences went to see was not an act of impersonation but precisely this triumph of cast-iron personality over the haz-ards of life, desertion, betrayal, misunderstanding, and death.

When the tide of popular taste turned, it was the inde-structibility of the stars of the '20s and '30s, far more than their exaggerated makeup or their unfashionable clothes, that audiences laughed to scorn. Their mockery was mis-placed. These films embodied an eternal truth. Not merely on the screen but in life itself, the only way in which we can sur-vive and be seen to survive is by the dexterous use of a care-fully selected and patiently rehearsed set of mannerisms.

MISS GARBO

A critic has said of Miss Greta Garbo that in her pictures she always seemed to be the only member of the cast who had read the script to the bitter end. She was the only one who knew that it would all turn out badly. One might go fur-ther and say that tragedy was her element. The trashy material of most of her films was brought to life only when the moment arrived for her to deliver one of her lectures on hopeless love. This appeared to be the one subject which, though it is unlikely that she ever experienced it, appealed strongly to this actress's imagination. The voice for which everyone in the world—except one or two mean-spirited movie reviewers—had been waiting turned out, in Garbo's talkies, to be permanently charged with emotion. It was made for the throaty crooning of captionese. "I am so sorry for all the women that are not in love" (Inspiration). "To me love is only a little warmth in all this cold "(Romance). And of course, the greatest caption of all time: "Perhaps it is better that I live only in your heart, where nothing can stain our love." How heartrending that would have looked in Caslon Old Style type, white on black, with a drawing of a camellia in the bottom right-hand corner!

To realize fully the magnitude of this woman's life-style, we need only imagine how empty—indeed, how embarrassing—these words would sound issuing from the lips of any other movie actress. Audiences left her films in a trance of numbed acceptance, wondering vaguely why the world, which to the rest of humanity seemed such a jolly place, was not good enough for her.

I am warned that Sweden resents the opinion held by the rest of the world that suicide is its national style. It is a pity, for without it the country has no style at all. Nonetheless, to avoid causing the withdrawal of ambassadors, I will not put forward the suggestion that Miss Garbo's gloom was typically Swedish. We will consider her not geographically but in relation to history.

She came to California when the reign of Miss Gish appeared to be ended. Recent events have shown us that in fact this lady's reign never ends. She is a true exponent of lifestyle and has converted the career in which she set out into the profession of being.

Judged by the limited standard of Hollywood, however, her kingdom seemed to diminish. She represented sweetness and light, and from these two commodities the consumer appeal was passing rapidly. Someone had to be discovered who could win the love of several men in one film without in real life losing that of Mr. Mayer. Miss Garbo did this by fornicating liberally but with massive distaste. The love behind her was always carnal and revolting, the love ahead divine.

In *Anna Christie* she played the part of a prostitute and yet looked forward, if not with relish, at least with shakily founded hope, to being married to Mr. Charles Bickford. To modern moralists the argument of this film would seem perverse. Mr. Bickford agreed to accept Miss Christie only after she swore that she had never loved any of her customers in St. Paul. Nowadays this assertion would make disgusting a way of life that might otherwise be thought of as an interesting experience.

Even so Miss Garbo was the harbinger of the permissive society. Whatever happens to sex from now on, there will be no more divine women. Some clot left the greenhouse door open.

MISS DIETRICH

In the case of Miss Marlene Dietrich, the permissiveness that has now engulfed civilization went a step nearer the precipice. It was only natural that it should. She arrived later than Miss Garbo, stayed longer, and came from a country where the existence of sin was at least acknowledged. And the morality of her films would not have been subjected to quite so much scrutiny.

She was not a Goldwyn property. When she appeared in *Shanghai Express* she played the part of a white (or scarlet) woman drumming up yellow trade. Critics, claiming to be "reasonably broad-minded," were outraged. This was partly because in the eyes of the elders she had sunk lower, but also because she patently did not share Miss Christie's remorse for her past. She did her hair five different ways in one train journey and gave every impression of doing with great aplomb what she knew very well how to do. The sphinxlike quality that Mr. Josef von Sternberg imparted to her differed from that of other female stars. It was neither unearthly nor tragic. It was mocking. It held her within the great tradition, allowing audiences to read into her mask whatever secret yearnings they wished and to garland her neck with their dream as though she were a visitor to Polynesia, but this particular enigma variation was also an expedient.

When Miss Dietrich first arrived in California she was less sure of the American language than she later became. It was therefore best for her to murmur her veiled way through various captions with as little passion as possible.

Most of her strength seemed to go into the raising and lowering of her eyelashes. No wonder. They were at least an inch long.

By the time she finally ended her association with her mentor, her image was faultless. Quite rightly, she never made any dramatic alterations, even to her lighting. She feared to lose the love of Paramount—even of the whole world. To save her fabulous face and nod distantly to changing fashions, she extended the immaculate mockery that she habitually lavished on men to include the movie industry itself.

In a film called *Seven Sinners* Miss Dietrich played a woman so wicked that even her street clothes were backless. Mr. Broderick Crawford had to pummel her into agreeing not to drag the fair name of Mr. John Wayne in the dust by marrying him. Convinced, she sailed away from Singapore to higher heels and thicker marabou. In the last moments of this picture we see her asking the ship's doctor for a cigarette. "You're a real pal, Doc," she says. This line is clearly not a caption, and another actress might have accompanied the words with a playful punch on the biceps, but not the imperturbable Miss Dietrich. She murmurs the words languorously, as though she were in bed with the doctor, and turns toward him a face half-shrouded by a diagonal eye veil. The lashes of one eye poke through the black net like arms of mute appeal; in the other is the famous equivocal expression. In spite of the jarring American slang, no breach of style has been permitted. Glamour *omnia vincit.*

MISS WEST

Miss Mae West was a conspicuously round woman in a very square industry.

Nevertheless, at the start of the 1930s, she took to Hollywood like a duck to drakes. In that far-off age there was still a noticeable difference between the sexes, and studio heads catered almost exclusively to what they considered to be women's tastes in entertainment. Sensual pleasure was veiled by prudery or sentimentality. Miss West was guilty of neither of these sins. Her sense of humor would at that time have been described as masculine; it was founded on superb detachment. In her day the vogue was for making fun of intimate relationships between men and women by presenting one or both parties as hideous, old, or in some other way ill-equipped for love. But this unpleasant ploy only ridicules the unfortunate. Miss West struck with faultless aim at the very heart of the matter; she lampooned sex.

Almost from the beginning of her movie career (short if you exclude the horrible *Myra Breckinridge,* she imposed upon her pictures not only her unique view of the human comedy but also her own method of photographing it. Before her reign, almost all wisecracks ended with an abrupt cut corresponding with the blackout that followed the punch lines of old-fashioned revue sketches. Miss West insisted that she be shown walking–nay, sailing–away from her deflated victims, thus producing a joke upon a joke.

Her success seems all the more remarkable if we remember that it occurred when Wall Street–when the entire Western world–was tottering. Through those dark days she kept Paramount solvent single-handedly, though doubtless the lady herself would say that hands were not all that she employed.

Now that she is gone we shall never be sure how she achieved her singularly personal triumph in a business where traditionally so many people have a finger in the pie, to say nothing of a hand in the cookie jar. If charisma is the ability to persuade without the use of logic, then it was probably by this elusive power that Miss West ruled with such apparent ease her chosen domain.

MISS CRAWFORD

There is a very special glow which surrounds people who have succeeded in synthesizing their professional and personal lives. Joan Crawford appeared in any number of movies in which she rose from rags to riches, and in real life she finally married Mr. Pepsi-Cola. She had all the luck in the world, because he died. This meant that she could enter herself into the boardroom of that vast worldwide empire, where presumably she said, "Who told *you* to read the minutes?" just as she'd done in all her movies.

I saw Joan Crawford in front of the National Film Theatre. A car as long as the Thames drew up, and from it stepped those two now-famous children. They stood in the lobby looking bewildered, and no wonder, for after about three minutes Miss Crawford came out of the same car and kissed the children as though she hadn't seen them for months. I had gone up a few steps in order to have a really good view, and for a second she saw me from those great alligator eyes. It felt as if my image were being burned on the wall behind me. She was incandescent with belief in herself.

MR. BRANDO

In that happy, far-off time when there was a difference between the sexes, it was more difficult to be a male than a female star. The dubious profession of acting was thought to foster vanity–a sin forgiven (sometimes even encouraged) in women. As we know from witnessing Mr. Kenneth Russell's film about Signor Valentino, cinema technicians considered all actors effete or worse, but it was possible to avoid suspicion by riding a horse or carrying a gun. Then the writings of Mr. Tennessee Williams came to the notice of Hollywood, and the image of manliness became more extreme. All this dramatist's early plays are about women brought deliciously low by their sexual appetites. His heroines are really men in drag, and therefore their lovers are brutes. That is how the world first saw Mr. Brando–as a desirable oaf, a furless Mr. Kong.

From this highly original role he emerged slowly through *The Fugitive Kind* to the well-dressed, fully articulate *Ugly American,* but he has never been able completely to scrape from his noble face the acid spittle of the critics. When he played Mr. Anthony in *Julius Caesar,* the English complained that he had an American accent. Since no one was speaking Roman, why did this matter? He was the only actor ever to recite Mr. Shakespeare's verse as though it were normal speech.

Last Tango in Paris was universally regarded as a dirty joke, whereas in fact it was a tragic film elevated to greatness by the performance of its star. *The Godfather* fared better. It was highly praised, but no one remarked that if Mr. Brando had for a moment rolled his eyes, bared his teeth, or in any way behaved like a gangster, the whole film would have become worthless. It was good because he showed us a patriarch doing his best for relatives whom he despised—a man degraded by the horrors of family life.

Apart from Mr. Emil Jannings, Mr. Brando was the greatest screen personality the movies have produced. Now he has gone into science fiction, which is where actors go when they die. Why was he murdered?

MISS GARLAND

A pleasant feeling is always generated by the demise of a celebrity. The occasion gives us nonentities a lot to discuss, and it provides us with situations upon which to lavish those tears which our sons and our lovers find embarrassing and try to prevent us from shedding. It also proves to the envious that, ultimately, the stars are only our equals, or we theirs if we can just find a significant way to die.

The worship of Miss Judy Garland has turned out to be more peculiar and less ephemeral than this customary public interest. It started with her failure. On the first day of shooting *Annie Get Your Gun,* Miss Garland was replaced by Miss Hutton. The world shook. It was not possible to think that the star of so many nice, healthy movies had done anything wrong, so she became a self-evident victim. From that moment onward, she attracted the homosexual vote. These men did not so much champion her cause as wallow in her defeat.

How did Miss Garland race so far ahead of her nearest competitors in the Degradation Stakes? Miss Edith Piaf might have been a rival but she was disqualified; she was French, and being French is a form of degradation in itself. A more edifying parallel can be drawn between Miss Garland and Mrs. Arthur Miller. All rights to the soul of this unfortunate woman have been bought up by Mr. Norman Mailer. One therefore hesitates to mention the name of Miss Monroe, but it can at least safely be said that she too was wracked by the lust for reassurance. She also became a cause for anxiety among her coworkers, but not an object of contempt like Miss Garland did, according to Mr. Dirk Bogarde, who was her costar in *I Could Go On Singing*. What prevented Miss Monroe from sinking to the lowest level of abjection was her looks. Even when all was lost, she remained beautiful. Miss Garland, on the other hand, totally lacked glamour. When I first saw *The Wizard of Oz,* I was appalled by her lack of prettiness, by her bulging eyes, her short neck. In her later films she offset her plainness by weaving into her screen image an element of self-mockery, but she never became alluring. Indeed, she was hardly a woman; I do not recall ever seeing her half-naked or even in a transparent negligee.

This disadvantage gradually became one of her assets. She never inspired envy. No one's eyes narrowed or became green when they watched her win the love of Mr. Mickey Rooney. In fact, the world *gave* her Mr. Rooney unconditionally.

Miss Garland's ambitions on the screen were exceptionally modest, while in real life the world demanded such a lot of her. I think it was the combination of these two factors that raised this unhappy song-and-dance girl to be the patron saint of a group of men who, however much they differ in other respects, are united in the idea that they are persecuted by a heartless world.

FRANCES

Of course, there must be film people who get up, go to work, return home, write to their mothers, and generally live like the rest of us, but the histories of these well-behaved individuals never reach the bookshops. Inevitably we form the impression that if her looks or her luck or the ambitions of her mother raise a girl to a level from which she can clearly see the lamp of fame, she will dash herself against it until she breaks her wings and falls to a depth of degradation unimaginable to the more fortunate among us who are born plain and boring.

Miss Frances Farmer, whose story is somewhat sketchily told in the film *Frances,* was one of these beautiful but doomed young women.

We first see her reading to a group of startled parents and teachers in an end-of-term composition about the fact that there is no God. Even then, at the age of 16, she wears almost permanently the mocking, desperate smile of someone who at any moment may hit you.

She wins a prize and, later, a visit to Moscow and the disapproval of her hometown, Seattle. She is labeled a pinko, and her troubles begin. In spite of this, she goes to Hollywood and a few frames later is put under a seven-year contract by Paramount. Her head filled with the socialist rubbish preached by the detestable Mr. Clifford Odets and the Group Theater, she apparently imagined that she would have some control over the subject matter of the films in which she appeared. When she finds that this is by no means the case, she leaves Hollywood but is forced back by her studio chiefs, who make an example of her by humiliating her in every possible way. Under this treatment she becomes uncontrollable, strikes her dresser, resists arrest, and generally carries on in such a way that she ends up in a mental hospital.

A woman's place is in a home.

The film has been very carefully researched. The dialogue, the clothes, are just right, and I am told that the fights with the police are exactly like the newspaper photographs of these incidents taken at the time. The picture is very obliquely directed, but occasionally Miss Jessica Lange leaps out of the screen at you, as when she says to a gossip writer, "You're an intelligent man. Can't you find a way of earning a living that is less undignified?" In any case, she wins my personal Oscar because she spares herself nothing. If she ever writes the story of her life, it will be a catalogue of sprains, bruises, and abrasions. For almost half the entire length of the film, she is screaming, fighting, cursing. It is a remarkable performance that scorns the love not only of her friends, her employers, and her jailers in the movie, but also of the film's audience. In this sense, *Frances* is quite a different matter from *The Snake Pit*. There, Miss Olivia De Havilland, however bedraggled she became, retained the image of the butterfly on the wheel. (What would a butterfly be doing on a wheel?) By comparison, Miss Lange seems a clever, foulmouthed, and totally ungrateful hooligan. This means that the film is fascinating and horrifying but never sad.

In a way its power is also its weakness. Except when she is with her father, we hardly ever see the heroine being polite—let alone kind. Therefore, we keep asking ourselves, "What did she have that made her so instantly acceptable to the movie moguls?" At that time all the pretty girls in the world traveled to Southern California, so her mere appearance would never have been enough to recommend her. Did she make audiences laugh or cry or breathe deeply? We are never told; we only see her making everybody cringe.

Then, after repeated recapture by the authorities, after doses of shock treatment, after hours in a straitjacket, comes the brain operation. The surgeon explains to a hospital audience what he is about to do, how quick and how cheap the process is, but we are not shown the operation in full; we are cheated of the long-awaited climax. Perhaps I should report that at this juncture, several people left the cinema, but I felt that it was too late for tact; I needed to see the blood flow.

The film ends quietly on the other side of lobotomy. Miss Farmer is redeemed, wears the little black dress and pearls, and behaves with decorum. At this point Miss Lange should have looked a little thicker in the middle, but her acting cannot be criticized. She is polite but lifeless; we can tell that the mainspring is gone.

I think that the conclusion we must draw from this movie is obvious. All actresses should be lobotomized as soon as they are put under contract. It would save such a lot of anguish for them, for their agents, for their directors, and in spite of the surgeon's exorbitant fees, in the end it would save the studios a lot of money.

Throughout the film, the person I understood best was Miss Farmer's mother, superbly played by Miss Kim Stanley. At one moment she seized hold of her daughter and, in tones of exasperated amazement, cried out, "You had everything; you were a movie star." What the hell was it that Miss Farmer wanted?

I have since seen the television program entitled *Will There Really Be a Morning?* which is on the same theme. It lacked the glittering presence of Miss Lange and a certain visual melodrama that enlivened *Frances,* but its narrative line is much simpler, and the heroine is presented to the viewers so directly that even I, who would cut my wrists to be a movie star, understood some of her problems.

THE HUNGER

Fifty years ago, if you had told any girl–any nice girl–that she looked sexy, she would have slapped your face. Life was pleasant then. There was a lot of flirtation and very little fornication, or, if your interests lay elsewhere, there were a great many mysterious threats and very little murder. People lived largely in the mind and always seemed to have some adventure to which they could look forward.

Now all that has changed. Nay, everything has been reversed.

In the 1980s fulfillment precedes desire. This nasty state of affairs is reflected in many of our contemporary movies, or possibly it is caused by them.

Just such a film is *The Hunger;* it should have been called *The Glut.* It drips with blood and oozes sex.

I myself belong to Vampires Anonymous, and I can assure you that a vampire's life is not easy. After a while you need a fix every few hours. It is a little like being a diabetic but much more like being a drug addict; you can expect no sympathy from anybody—especially not from the police. On the credit side of this life-style is the fact that you become very rich. Miss Catherine Deneuve lives in a town house big enough to justify the installation of an elevator, and all the rooms are decorated in muted but perfect taste, with priceless works of art dotted about them. Presumably even 50 cents put into he capable hands of E. F. Hutton in the time of the pharaohs would yield a considerable yearly income by 1983. Apparently, you also become strong. When Mr. David Bowie grows too old to walk or even crawl, his hostess is able to carry him to the attic and place him in his coffin beside a few of his precursors with no obvious effort. She looked like a tired housekeeper taking an extra blanket to one of the guest rooms.

The disadvantages of vampirehood are that, while remaining a prey to hideous appetites, you cease to feel any emotion and are incapable, except when slitting somebody's throat, of making any swift movement. Miss Deneuve drifts about her house like an underwater swimmer. Indeed, *The Hunger* is like a vehicle for an unhealthy Esther Williams photographed not in her habitual bright blue swimming pool but in a badly kept canal.

The plot of *The Hunger,* if such there be, concerns a rich woman who spends her life giving strangely lethargic music lessons or bickering wanly with Mr. Bowie as though they were two touring actors filling in a Sunday afternoon in a provincial town. In flagrant defiance of the Trade Descriptions Act, she offers her victims everlasting life. They learn later that they have only been given three or four hundred years, at the end of which niggardly span they start to age at the rate of several days an hour. When we first meet Mr. Bowie, this process of disintegration has already begun.

Meanwhile, in another part of town, Miss Susan Sarandon is having a jolly time watching a small monkey turning into a skeleton. She is working on a cure for premature senility. Mr. Bowie hears of her researches and pays a visit to the hospital where she is employed. Here we encounter the film's only glimpse of reality. He sits all day in the waiting room, growing older by the minute; no one comes to his aid. In the very next sequence we are right back in our world of fantasy. Dr. Sarandon calls on him without mentioning money. A likely story! She meets Miss Deneuve and they become lovers. How much time passes it would be hard to guess, but one fine day there is an earthquake. The house rocks, the coffins in the attic burst open, and the living dead arise from the crumbling inertia to revenge themselves upon their hostess, who then also lapses into instant decay.

Why? How? What does it all mean?

I have demanded an explanation for these events from several people. So far, no satisfactory exegesis has been forthcoming.

However fantastic the premise upon which a movie is

based, nothing excuses illogicality. A good picture is a series of gloriously foregone conclusions–a moral crossword puzzle. A scenarist has only two weapons with which to conquer his public. These are suspense and surprise. A truly great screenwriter uses both. He warns his audience of impending danger, but when disaster strikes, he makes it worse than anyone could have foreseen though no more than his villains deserve. This will one day come to be known as the Hitchcock Principle. I cannot say that *The Hunger* obeys this precept.

The two leading ladies quite rightly do not act. They present their glorious bodies to the cameras, drift about the screen like sleepwalkers, and glow. They are incandescent with moral decay. The acting is done by one of Miss Deneuve's music students and by Mr. Bowie. The former brings to this bizarre story its few moments of innocent common sense. It is through her alone that we receive any idea of a bunch of weirdos living in secret isolation in the midst of the normal world. Mr. Bowie's performance is even more remarkable. While seeming to doze in a hypnotic trance, he manages to make us aware that beneath his mask he is sick, terrified, and consumed by an irreversible anguish.

Finally, far outshining any other asset this film may have is the charisma of its star. She is a very cool, upmarket vampire scorning to sleep in her coffin or wear joke-shop teeth. When I last saw her, in Mr. Roman Polanski's *Repulsion,* she was a pretty French girl. Now she is a sophisticated, superbly elegant American woman. The one thing I would not wish on my worst enemy is eternal life, but if anything could compensate anyone for having this appalling burden laid upon him, it would be the delight of being bitten by Miss Deneuve.

ERNESTO

This movie contains the most romantic love scene ever depicted on the screen. It is more poetic than Lord Tennyson's description of Mr. Lancelot's adultery with Mrs. Arthur, more lyrical than the duet sung by Lieutenant Pinkerton and Miss Fly, more beautiful than the famous kiss sculpted by Rodin.

The amorous sequence about which I am rhapsodizing takes place during the first 20 minutes of the film. Both aesthetically and for reasons of realism, this is too soon. The story never again reaches such a high level of intensity. Worse, the speed with which Ernesto and his lover arrange to consummate their desire makes the situation seem slightly facile. The boy is so young that he does not need to shave, while his lover is over 30; the boy is Jewish, whereas his friend is Italian; the boy is middle-class, but his friend is a manual laborer. These barriers would not be easy to cross even now, when all our values have collapsed. Seventy years ago they would have been impassable.

To some extent, the love scenes depend for their special quality on the photography. The laborer is extremely handsome but does not appear to have been technically idealized by soft-focus lenses and rosy lighting. The embrace can be seen to be sodomitic, but you-know-what is never shown. However, the essential luminosity of this sequence emanates from the acting of Mr. Placido.

In a sexual encounter there is a moment (which most people never experience) in which the orgasm is followed by a lull of sad but transcendental peace. It flows out of every pore of the body in a surge of gratitude to the love object. It is this blend of triumphant joy and humility that the actor manages to convey to his audience.

The picture *does* try to sell sex to us for more than it can ever be worth. Mr. Samperi, the director, can be accused of the same sentimentality that weakens Mr. Forster's novel *Maurice.* You cannot go and live forever in an English wood with a gardener (what would your mother say?), and similarly, there is no such thing as a romantic Italian laborer.

As this movie is called *Ernesto,* we do not really have the right to expect anything but what we are given. The picture is consistently well-acted, beautifully photographed in the green-gold light of a painting by Mr. Vermeer, and attractively costumed in the period of 1910. Nevertheless, I couldn't help longing for the narrative to be not about a young bourgeois's ignoble dash for cover, but about a beautiful Italian workman's broken heart. Because I was brought up on films featuring M. Jean Gabin, there are times when I thought the lover might stab his little friend. I would have liked that.

Quite often, when reviewing movies, I have found that apparently my heart was not in the right place, and I have known at least one other person who suffered from the same feeling of displacement. I took him to see *King Kong* (the first time round). During a dramatic episode in which a certain Miss Wray lay gibbering across Mr. Kong's wrist, my friend, in a voice shrill with irritation, cried out, "I can't think what he sees in her."

THE MOST EROTIC
MOVIE EVER MADE

When we hear a movie actress speak, she immediately acquires a nationality and, worse, a class. Her image becomes limited. She can no longer embody all our dreams. But in younger and happier days, when the films were silent, their stars had the power to wound the imagination beyond repair.

In the late 1920s all the most exciting pictures were made in Germany, many of them by Mr. Fritz Lang. He liked his women fatal and processed his actresses to fit this ideal. His greatest discovery was Miss Brigitte Helm, whom he put into *Metropolis,* the first science fiction movie ever made. In this movie the usual mad scientist captures her and with some rather glib use of electricity makes a robot in her likeness, except that the chromium Miss Helm has no soul, and one eye never shuts.

In the original version of this story, the robot does a pseudo-Egyptian dance, but from later copies this episode, presumably because it was thought too shocking, was cut and an alternative sequence was substituted, which in fact was infinitely more perverse.

An entirely male audience is seen staring intently at some silver theater curtains. Suddenly Miss Helm insinuates herself between the curtains. She is wearing a black satin dress which reaches up to her ears, down to her knuckles, and trails along the ground behind her. She divides the slit in her skirt just enough to reveal one thigh, from which she snatches a diamenté garter, which, with a darting cobra-like movement, she flings at her audience. At once a forest of hands springs up to catch it, and the sequence is over. In all it cannot have lasted more than a minute, but its impact was unforgettable. At that moment, Miss Helm looked like a large spider that had been dipped in melted sugar.

I cannot imagine anything more alluring.

PART SEVEN

In which Mr. Crisp confronts

TRAVEL

SUMMER EXHIBITION

People who cannot expect any alteration in their lives to be wrought by a deepening understanding either of themselves or of their friends must seek variety from external sources. Their chief hope seems to rest in changes of climate. These mysteriously produce corresponding differences in morality, and summer, at least, provokes a laxity that, in a cooler season, tends to remain dormant.

Many long, dark years ago, the cover of *The New Yorker* displayed a picture of a middle-aged lady of high degree standing before a coal fire with her skirts raised behind her sufficiently to warm the backs of her legs. The humor of the painting lay in the hint of sensuality in the character of a woman accustomed to cluttered—nay, suffocating—respectability.

Our reaction would have passed from gentle amusement to shocked incredulity had she been depicted rolling on a towel and, with a palmful of almond oil and sleek, self-loving caresses, redistributing the sweat on her half-naked body. Yet elsewhere than in a baronial hall such behavior became for many at another season of the year a daily public occurrence. Indeed, for months on end, all other activities had to be scheduled to accommodate it.

In my childhood, as a solemn duty, my mother used to take me to the summer exhibitions of the Royal Academy. One year a picture was hung called *The City of Dreams*. Even I—then, as now, insular to the edge of agoraphobia—knew this meant Monte Carlo. Of course, half the fantasies that were focused on that metropolis concerned defeating with one's pet system the inscrutable croupiers, but it was also true that longings for romance swam like fireflies through the night air round the casino. In fact, if you wanted to win the love of a Latin prince or even to arouse the cupidity of a gigolo, the right thing to do was to remain no pinker than the Parthenon. It would have been so easy for women to enjoy the warmth of a southern clime without torturing themselves to the color of a basted chicken, but a policy of moderation was never adopted. It was essential to take back to England proof that one had not merely been wind-bathing in Bournemouth. Only those people who could flaunt a deep tan before the envious eyes of their poorer relatives were able to demonstrate beyond all reasonable doubt that their fathers or husbands could afford to send them abroad.

To avoid the charge of vulgarity, no mention was ever made of the real reason for having worked so single-mindedly upon an epidermic metamorphosis. Instead it was always claimed that prolonged exposure to the rays of the sun was health-giving. It was, of course, no such thing. The skin darkens to protect the body from too much sunlight—and excess of vitamin D. Furthermore, the practice of passing every year from snow white in winter to mahogany color in summer eventually gives the skin the texture of rhinoceros hide.

The human body is not so much the temple of Aphrodite as a poorly designed gravity-resisting mechanism in constant danger of going wrong. We have only to watch a barefoot bather crossing stony ground to realize how hideously vulnerable we all are–to regret the mistake we made in abandoning our hooves and our fur. Neither stripping nor any of the other devices mentioned above rendered the denizens of the seashore any prettier, but this did not matter. It is not only people with good figures who display them. In the days of the miniskirt, the shortest garments of all seemed usually to be worn by girls the widest part of whose legs was their knees. *Beauty is in the eye of the possessor.*

AUSTRALIA AND HOW TO CURE IT

I am standing innocently in my hotel room looking down at the doll's-house churches nestling among the skyscrapers that are a feature of the city of Brisbane. The telephone bell rings. My caller explains that he is attending a school in which his class has been told to write an essay about a television documentary program showing my arrival in Australia. This piece of information is in itself astounding. In England no teacher would set his pupils such a task unless he were more interested in publicity than a steady job.

With what argument could he convince a board of governors that a subject so scandalous was merely a test of syntax and punctuation?

I realize instantly that, having still nine weeks to do in Australia, I must not figure in a sixth-form essay beginning:

"When I met Mr. Crisp in his hotel bedroom…" To avoid this, I ask my visitor to accompany me to the theater at which, in an hour's time, I am to perform. I think that my dressing room will provide a marginally less questionable venue. As I go onto the stage in the clothes in which I walk through the streets, there will be no ooh-la-la behind an inadequate screen. Backstage I answer all the young man's questions without, I hope, saying anything which, if repeated by him, will cause either his father or his headmaster any alarm.

Nevertheless, our conversation is by no means humdrum. "My friends say that you're a slob," my interrogator remarks without hostility. He has noticed that my shirt is held together with a safety pin. I agree, and the interview passes pleasantly

Had he known it, it was a good night; there are times when I seem to be wearing chain armor.

In Melbourne I stood in the entrance to a cinema waiting for a taxi. Near at hand, two young men discussed whether they had or had not seen me on television a few days earlier. When they decided that they had, one of them approached me and shook my hand. After an exchange of pleasantries, he says, "So you're homosexual. Big deal." If these words were intended to mock anybody, they were aimed not at me but at the world. The phrase expressed the same liberality, the same blandness as that evinced by the previous adolescent– but in shorthand.

Everywhere you go in Australia, once it is known that you come from England, you are asked what you think of the place and its inhabitants. The question is put in a slightly hesitant voice as though expecting a rebuff. On one occasion I was openly invited to consider the whole continent a cultural desert. I am the wrong kind of person to bombard with this kind of interrogation; to me, culture is any television program too boring to be advertised as entertainment. I am more interested in sophistication. If this is the quality that Australians feel they lack, they need have no fear. They have only to wait for the young men mentioned above to grow up.

What makes this national self-doubt the more disturbing is that it is felt in a land where happiness (for which culture is a poor substitute) grows on trees. The streets are paved with opals and, even in Newcastle, laughingly called "soot city" by my guide, the air is as bright as diamonds. There and everywhere else in this earthly paradise, it is never colder than an English spring; the houses are as clean as they were painted; the vegetation is as green as in an everlasting May and in places covered with camellias as big as cabbages. In the cities the thoroughfares are wide and lined with trees as graceful as birches. Furthermore, in keeping with this setting, everyone is rich; the trains are empty but the airplanes are full–chiefly of men carrying in plastic covers their board-meeting suits.

Why then have the denizens of this Elysium become a nation of Madame Butterflies, forever standing by the shore with their eyes focused on the far horizon? Why is it that, when you arrive at any airport, it is as though you had come to save the entire continent (even at 7 in the morning)?

I pointed out to a reporter the fact that Sydney is no further from New York than New York from Sydney. Reluctantly she agreed.

When trouble comes England will lie flat on its belly in the dust of humiliation trying to avoid being caught in cross fire exchanged by two giants, both of whom it has made the mistake of trying to placate. Then, at last, Australia will realize that being 13,000 miles from the madding crowd was a hidden asset.

Of course, it is not impossible that all this self-deprecation is just another example of the sophistication manifested by my schoolboys. It may be a polite ruse intended to prevent foreigners from feeling that they have lost face in the presence of such coast-to-coast prosperity.

If, on the contrary, this continental malaise is real, I have a simple remedy to offer. It is purely a convention that north is at the top of all our maps. Why do we not, for the next hundred years at least, agree to print our atlases the other way up? Then Australia would no longer occupy the invidious place of an anthropological footnote. Indeed, it would be the opening paragraph to the history of the world.

I VISIT THE COLONIES

If your fare is being paid by others, it is likely that you will travel not so much to see as to be seen. You will not be taken to well-known beauty spots but will be unceremoniously rushed by photographers to ruined dance halls and deserted wharves, where it is hoped that an unusual background will do something for your ignoble profile. Mountains, lakes, cathedrals you will look at in the way that most people watch television—by default; your judgments, therefore, are apt to be generalized.

Last year, on my first visit to New York, I stayed in the

Drake Hotel as a guest of Mr. Michael Bennett. I formed the opinion that everyone in America was rich and, which is more to the point, generous. When I returned to my native land, I told all my friends that they would need to take no money with them, as they would be able to drift forward on a tide of transatlantic kindness. This year my manager and I stayed in the Chelsea Hotel and decided that everyone was poor and discontented. The day after we arrived, there was a robbery; the following afternoon, a fire. The inmates brought their cats downstairs and sat in the hideous lobby talking airily of this and that without so much as a mention of the flames. Thirty-six hours later there was a murder. At last a little curiosity was evinced. As the corpse was carried into the street, a man kept pace with the foremost stretcher-bearer in order to question him.

"How did she die?"

"Stabbed."

"How often?"

The day after this we left.

We went to Chicago, to find our preconceptions of that city totally reversed. Between its stately homes lie wide streets lined with sunny, yellowing trees beneath which couples stroll at leisure. The hotel in which we stayed–the Ambassador–is the most beautiful that I have ever entered.

When, as travelogues used to say, we bade farewell to this place of captivating beauty, we flew to Boston. I have always said that New York was like heaven; Boston, on the contrary, I would describe as being like home–not only in appearance but in fact. For instance, if you arrive there in a fainting condition and ask for breakfast to be brought to your room, you are warned that there will be two and a half hours' delay.

"But by then it will be lunchtime."

"That's correct, sir."

"Then should I, perhaps, order lunch?

"It might be as well, sir."

Mercifully, on this occasion sustenance arrived in an hour and a half.

If the distance between the stars is so great that it is convenient to measure it in light-years, then the money spent by my sponsors on hotel bills should be reckoned in light-dollars, but in spite of my vulgar delight at suddenly living in reckless splendor after nearly 40 years spent in one room in London, I cannot deny that I am made extremely uneasy by hotels. I do not remember who it was that said foreign travel was largely a matter of getting used to the plumbing, but I can now endorse that statement. Many times I have scalded myself before remembering that in America taps turn off in a clockwise direction; often panic has raged through my feeble frame while I searched for the apparatus that allows the bathwater to run away and which at length turned out to be situated outside the bath and not inside it as in England. Even simple light switches operate in reverse.

I am frightened not only by the gadgets with which hotel bedrooms bristle; I also fear the staff, who detect at once that I am an upstart–an impression that overtipping only serves to confirm. I find–and this I did not realize until I was halfway through my long journey–that I need to spend a considerable amount of time alone and, worse, that I have to be certain my solitude will not be interrupted. I cannot sit happily in my hotel room if I know that at an unspecified time a cleaner will arrive to "do" it. The more glorious the hotel, the greater this problem becomes. In the Beverly Hills Hotel, someone arrives at twilight to perform the solemn ritual of removing the counterpane from the bed. This meant that from dawn till dusk, I remained in a state of suppressed anxiety. One evening I rejected this service, only to find a moment later that a note stating what I had done had been pushed under the door. I took this to be a reproach and, consequently, felt guilty for the rest of the night.

When I was being wafted through the streets of Los Angeles, I had hardly leaned back in his taxi before the driver asked if I was an actor. I told him that I was in the profession of being. Without hesitation, he replied, "I do a bit of that in my spare time." When you receive such a response as this, it is impossible to strike from your heart the desire to live forever in the Islands of the Blessed.

England is a haven for the very old, the very young, and anyone who feels that he is not fully equipped to live. Britain's slow pace, its tolerance, its minimum-risk policies, and its mild climate make it the natural setting for losers. This is the terrain that, after 70 years of stubborn insularity, I am struggling to leave. My friends warn me that if I succeed in taking up residence in America, I shall be hit over the head by strangers as incessantly as if I were a punching bag. I try to explain that, at least until it actually happens, it is worth it. Being in New York is like bathing in soda water; the scrotum tingles as you walk through those canyons of steel and glass in which everyone seems to be engaged in some activity that he finds exciting or hurrying toward someone he loves. As all Englishmen say on their return home, "America is more like the movies than you ever dreamed."

BLOOMINGDALE'S VS. HARRODS

I seldom buy anything for myself—it's much too embarrassing. (In fact, I've found that if you compliment people judiciously, they will give you as many clothes as you need. E.g.: "Oh, are you *still* wearing that? No, no, it's *very* nice . . .") Nevertheless, during the week before Christmas I went to Mr. and Mrs. Bloomingdale's establishment to see how the other half gives. The answer is abundantly.

I was much impressed. Shopping in Harrods is a hushed, awesome experience, like attending divine worship in a cathedral. By comparison, the American equivalent, despite the size of the building, was positively cozy. Perhaps the overall dimensions of the place seemed less because of the vastness of some of its more bizarre contents, such as fake giraffe heads, life-size or worse, and a papier-mâche armadillo about three feet long. Moreover, the saleswomen were friendlier. One of them gave me a bottle of scent—presumably in a spirit of skittish experimentation. The biggest surprise of all, however, was finding, in the dress department, that a sale was in progress. During an English December, everything becomes dearer as well as colder, and at Christmastime it isn't the thought that counts, it's the money.

ON BEING ENGLISH IN NEW YORK

It seems that in the United States, Englishmen are regarded as pets, like budgies, that can almost speak American. To this may be added that if you seem to be even vaguely connected with show business, you become sacred.

I saw this most vividly when I was invited to visit the Church of the Beloved Disciple, on West 14th Street. I arrived to find an anniversary celebration in progress and, to my amazement, was asked to say a few words to the congregation. After the service, I was a guest at a huge banquet for about 150 parishioners, some of whom kissed me as though I were a relic (of the past?). Although I was acutely aware that my right to be present at such an event and in such a place was dubious, I greatly enjoyed myself. I was delighted to see so much evidence of genuine happiness and so little of that hysteria that traditionally characterizes gatherings of "gay" people.

In Sardi's, however, there is more squeaking, more embracing, more waving, more darting from table to table, than anywhere else on earth. The proprietor of an English establishment where such "goings-on" occurred once would find some way of preventing their ever happening again. If he did not, his staff would leave. Here the waiters do not look even faintly ruffled. They never have a clear run from any table to the kitchens, but with their trays held high over their heads, they wait patiently, looking down in mercy while the divine children flit past them.

Whether I am with slaves of the media or ordinary mortals, their attitude is frank but never indiscreet. All questions allow for a little evasion if it is feared that a direct answer might embarrass either them or me. While being very grateful for the gentleness with which I am everywhere treated, I am, of course, aware that it may in part be because I am a guest of America. Things might be different if I were a native and it were thought that the reputation of the United States could be tarnished by my odd behavior.

My presence here is bandwagon stuff, and my sponsor wishes it to remain so. While this metaphorical vehicle continues to roll, I shall never experience ordinary life. This fact causes me no concern because I never have. At first this was due to the permissiveness of English society; now it is due to the sanctifying properties of television. I am conscious that so long as you remain even vaguely recognizable, people are never going to be with you; they are always in your presence. There will be no conversation–only cozy inquisition. The effect of this on me is that I no longer walk through the streets scorning strangers before they can scorn me; nowadays in public I perpetually wear an expression of fatuous affability.

ON RIDING TRAINS

In the days when I was only English, I walked from London toward Scotland, covering 30 miles a day for nine days, until my ankles became the size of other people's thighs. Many years later I flew to Australia, remaining in the same seat in the same plane almost continuously for 24 hours, 16 of which were night. Both forms of locomotion, though so different, yielded an interesting form of agony. Train journeys do not possess this asset. Nowadays they cannot even boast of any comforting squalor.

Until a few years ago, in Britain at least, if you flung yourself into your seat with any kind of abandon, a cloud of acrid dust rose about you, and absolutely nothing could be seen through the windows because they were so thickly coated with grime. Recently even these reminders of home have disappeared. Once you are on it, a train has no danger and no glamour.

Perhaps for this reason, the English station staff feels no obligation to treat you with civility. Should you be unwise enough to ask an official if there will soon be a train to London, he is likely to reply, "There might be if you went onto the right platform."

In Britain service is considered to be the same thing as servility, and as such, if you have spent a long time in the quaint occupation of ruling the waves, it is almost certain to prove tiresome. Moreover, the English are reluctant to pander to fools. I can't think why; it is one of the easiest occupations available. By contrast with railway officials, the personnel of airlines is inexhaustibly courteous, though that may be in part because their customers are paying so much more. Some airlines offer their customers forms that invite criticism. No railway would be so rash as to do that.

American railways seem vastly different from their English counterparts, but I should add that I have only made short journeys, from New York to Philadelphia and to New Haven. I would like to travel a greater distance, although I have been warned that the experience is absolute hell. I doubt that a transcontinental journey at ground level would be as irksome to me as it appears to others. I have spent 35 years as an art school model; this is a life of significant waiting without any hope of reaching a destination. Keeping still has become natural to me.

Apart from railing against the enforced inertia of train journeys, people utter no panegyrics about the scenery through which they pass; they only have hideous tales to tell about fellow passengers. These stories worry me because I have always felt that when we say of a stranger that he is tedious, it is ourselves that we criticize. Only a lie is boring.

On a long train journey we ought, therefore, to present ourselves to the other people in our coach as a wide-open, indestructible vessel into which the acids of truth can safely be poured. We should become for the time like psychoanalysts, making those sitting opposite feel that nothing they can say will shock us or provoke scorn. Travelers are often advised to take a long book on their journeys, but who would devote his attention to a book which will always be at hand when he can turn the dog-eared pages of a total stranger whom he may never meet again?

A little old lady sitting opposite me in an otherwise empty coach said, "...and then, after 25 years, my husband died." I was just about to look gravely at the floor between us when she added, "And oh, the relief." I would travel from Moscow to Vladivostok to hear a remark like that.

PART EIGHT

MR. CRISP'S RECORD
OF EMPLOYMENT

At work I never once understood what I was doing. In theory (in my first job) I was employed as an engineer's tracer. This was one of the many kinds of work at which I could never hope to be proficient. Accuracy is alien to my nature. Many years later a woman asked me what a "point" was. When I told her it was a 72nd part of an inch, she said, "But there isn't such a thing, really. Is there?" That is what I have always secretly thought. When I was given plans to trace, I copied the mistakes as well as the revisions, and neither of them properly; when I was told to transfer the position of electric pylons from one map to another, I did so with such a jolly laugh that construction men telephoned from distant shires to ask what on earth was going on at head office. If any housewife has a pylon among her rosebushes, if any country clergyman has a pylon sticking up through his church roof, if any borough surveyor has a pylon blocking his main thoroughfare, may she or he read here that I apologize. May it comfort them to know that I was happy.

My next job, like my first, was found for me by my mother. Digging ever deeper through older and older strata of friendship, she had unearthed the wife of a publisher whom we had all known in Sutton. (I had been to one of their hateful parties, during which rather than play games in which somebody had to kiss somebody, I had sat in another room and played patience with cards which I had had the forethought to bring with me.) My mother, in a fragment of the voluminous correspondence which, now that she lived in farthest Devonshire, was her chief hobby, pleaded with this woman, who nagged her husband, who coerced a printing firm with whom he did a lot of business to employ me in their art department.

I was not a success. I sat in an upper room and tried to adapt myself to the whims of a man so moody that most days passed in a silence unbroken even by greeting or valediction. On others he danced and sang with such vigor that, even if there had been any work to which my talents were equal, I could not have done it. The swinging of the lamps and the shaking of the floor would have prevented me. Some of his moodiness was, I think, due to his red hair, but more was caused by the burden that he carried on my behalf. As the head of our department, one of his duties was to take whatever work I did downstairs to the directors and explain it if he could. Doing this always brought down upon him humiliations that he could hardly bear. As a commercial artist, I was as hopeless as I had been as a tracer. Indeed, the qualifications were the same for both occupations—a slow pulse, good eyesight, and a minimum of ideas. The word "slick," now a term of contempt, was then the highest praise. In all the long dark years that I was in or on the fringe of advertising, my work never attained any noticeable degree of this quality of high gloss. I was always compelled to spend hours retouching my lettering and hours more retouching the retouching until the paper was embossed with white paint. The words I had written could only be read by the blind.

After a year of watching me doing this, the red-haired artist gave notice. As he left, he said, "I feel I ought to say something—give you some advice—but the thing for you to do is to carry on just the way you do now. You're as meek as a bloody lamb, but down there"—he jerked his 15-amp hair toward the floor, meaning in the boardroom, not in hell—"they know you don't care a damn about any of them and there's just nothing they can do about it."

He was wrong. I liked the directors; I had arranged to do so. I was secretly shocked to see stalking toward me naked what in my first job I had only seen heavily veiled—the senseless and implacable hatred that workers feel for their employers. This hostility was something to which I never grew accustomed. In my whole life, the only relationships with individuals (as opposed to crowds) that I took seriously were those that I managed to establish with the people for whom I worked. They paid me, and this raised them higher in my esteem than any amount of praise or protestation of affection ever could. In return I was their slave. To the amazement and sometimes the disgust of my coworkers in various studios, I never attempted to introduce any quality into my work that might be over the head of my boss. Nay, I executed drawings that I knew to be of the utmost banality with positive gusto, for whatever is done for money is sacred.

I felt that commercial art might become a permanent means of getting by. Being employed by the electrical engineers had only taught me how to ask where the gentlemen's lavatory was without blushing. Now I was learning something which might be really useful. I never thought of work as something that would one day earn me a lot of money. Squalor was my natural setting. I did not hope that a job would extend me to the limit of my talents. I hadn't any. What I wanted to wrest from regular employment was something with which to bargain with the heterosexual world for acceptance as a homosexual. This evangelical zeal was the real motive for everything I did. It would subside for a while and then flare up again—especially if my employer had recently called me into his office and made another attempt to coerce me into altering my appearance. Without looking at me, and moving the papers on his desk from side to side, he would say, "Fact of the matter is we don't particularly like employing people with plucked eyebrows and pointed fingernails." For a week or two my eyebrows, which usually marched across my forehead in single file, were allowed to form fours, and the style of my fingernails was changed from Gothic to Norman.

Surprisingly, I was not dismissed. On the contrary, the day came when I was given an assistant. Thinking only of the havoc that an extra two pounds in wages would wreak on the firm's economy, I at first protested at this daring expansion. The directors, laughing heartily, pointed out how inconvenient it would be for them if, while I was the only member of the art department, I were to become ill or get run over by a bus. I asked them to provide me with a female assistant. I foresaw that there would be mutiny if a man were ever placed in a position where he had to do as I said. Whether my

employers saw the sense of this I never knew, but they pan-
dered to my whim and engaged a charming girl, with whom
I worked happily for about a year. This was the first time I
had ever been in the position of a master instead of a slave. I
tried to behave with the utmost tact so as not to inflict on my
assistant any of the humiliations that had been heaped on
me. One day, however, presumably because of some special
pressure of work, when she held a drawing up for my ap-
proval, I said, "Yes. That's all right but the feet are bad." No
sooner had these harsh words passed my momentarily un-
guarded lips than I hastened to soften their directness with
chivalrous obliquities. "What I meant was," I began, "that
certain superficial critics might say–" At this point she cut me
short. "Thank God," she sighed. "You've said what you really
mean at last."

While I had not been watching, a number of tiny studios
had sprung up at the tops of narrow buildings in Fleet Street
and Chancery Lane. They had rather intimidating names like
The Twentieth Century Advertising Service or The New London Studios. If I burst into any of these offices, I usually found
two people playing table tennis in a nest of dirty teacups and
the crumpled drawings of forgotten art students.

During the next two winters I worked in some of these studios, whose staff could hardly be seen with the naked eye. In
the summer the tide of advertising always mysteriously re-
ceded, leaving all firms but those with the deepest roots high
and dry. In this period of drought someone from all these
smaller concerns had to be asked to leave. This was always
me. My feelings on being dismissed were a mixture of indig-

nation and relief. By the time I was 28, I had tired of this experience. I easily found a way of preventing its recurrence. I gave up work.

I became a freelance commercial artist.

I cannot claim that from this moment I was always happy, but from the age of 28, I never did for long anything that I didn't want to do—except grow old.

For anyone whose appearance is highly eccentric, it is usually first meetings that are a special ordeal. In the days when I had looked for regular employment I had only the initial interview for each job to negotiate. Now that I was freelancing, I had to face several such challenges every week. Since I depended for my livelihood on the goodwill of whomever I had come to see, these situations needed to be handled with much greater care than confrontations with strangers in the street. I found it necessary to develop a technique for being interviewed. This came into operation the moment I arrived at the reception desk. It began with not evincing any surprise as all the office boys fled through the doors nearest to them, firstly in order to fall about the corridors laughing without restraint and secondly so that they might spread to distant floors of the building the news of my advent. Then, while I waited for my appointment, I had to invent some artificial occupation for my attention so that it would seem natural for me not to look up as each member of the staff, carrying a meaningless piece of paper, came to speak to the receptionist. Finally, there was the interview itself. At the start of this I must, by what actors call some piece of "business," allow my client a good look at me while I was not looking at him. I did not always succeed in giving him time to put his eyes back in his head before I turned my gaze upon him.

Once the initial shock of seeing me had worn off, my interviewer was sometimes so relieved to find that I was not actually mad or even in any other way unconventional that he gave me work out of simple gratitude.

While I lived in Belgravia, two new ways of supplementing my fitful income from commercial art presented themselves. The first of these was writing, at which so far I had never had the least success. The Blandford Press, for whom I had often designed a book jacket or laid out an advertisement in one of their magazines, suggested that I should write a book about window dressing. I had never though of doing this because I knew nothing about the subject. The publishers did not think that this was any handicap, so I flung myself upon the project with all my half-starved weight and quickly wrote 30,000 words. I had only one idea to put forward–that in any visual field, maximum interest lies at the point of maximum contrast. After several shaky years the book sold out its edition. This only proves once more that people will pay to read what they already know.

The other profession in at the door of which I desperately thrust my lacquered toe was tap dancing. My landlady did not want pupils who wished to learn other forms of dancing than ballet to be turned away for lack of a fully equipped staff of experts. This was another subject of which I was totally ignorant, though this weakness never came to light. Only one student with tap dancing in mind ever turned up, and she was a beginner. I taught her by keeping one tap ahead at each lesson. The occupants of the workshop below had to endure a noise overhead like an African hailstorm beating on a tin roof, while I hastily practiced what I had just been taught before my pupil arrived to learn it. The steps were not made any easier for either of us by the clearly audible curses from below. To those poor workmen peace only came with the outbreak of war.

When war was declared I went out and bought two pounds of henna.

A letter requiring my appearance before a medical board reached me in the first April of the war. This was early, for I was already, in fact, 30 years old, but when, some time back, people had called at the mews to ask impertinent questions about my sex and age, I had stated that I was 25. I had not done this because I was eager to denounce a monstrous tyranny but to bring nearer the moment when the problem of how to avoid starvation would be taken out of my hands. Many of my friends were able to find work in camouflage. This seemed an unlikely way for me to earn a living. My function in life was rather to render what was already clear blindingly conspicuous. In spite of the frantic efforts I had made in so many directions to fortify myself against destitution, in a national emergency it transpired that I was utterly useless. It was almost enthusiastically that I set out for the drill hall in the middle of Kingston to which I had been summoned.

I was fully prepared to march at the head of my men, an

occupation in which I had had considerable practice, but the authorities were not having any of that. The moment I stood naked before the first doctor, he collapsed. I was surprised. My appearance was at half mast. I wore no makeup and my hair was hardly more than hooligan length. Many of my friends on seeing me thus would have cried out, "Whatever's happened to you?" but of course my hair was still crimson from having been persistently hennaed for seven years, and though my eyebrows were no longer in Indian file, it was obvious that they had been habitually plucked. These and other manifestations of effeminacy disturbed the board deeply.

I was totally exempt.

Working for the movies was the first job I ever wanted to do for reasons other than to show I could. For once, though I was prepared to accept defeat, I did not intend to embrace it. I wanted to be what would now be described as the Saul Bass of British movies and, to this end, I abandoned for a moment my existentialist posture. I applied for and, to my amazement, obtained a job in Studio Film Laboratories. This was a mistake. I was not able to flit from room to room learning the secret of the celluloid universe. I was confined to the art department, where, even if my ineptitude had not almost immediately been unmasked, I do not think I would have lasted long. My presence caused agony to the head of the studio. From lifelong habit I called him "Sir," never noticing that every time I did so he winced. Also, after a few weeks, he became aware that other members of his staff had learned by heart and were starting to use the detestable curlicues with which my discourse was decorated—nay, cluttered—and which later came to be called Crisperanto.

Within nine months I had once again been given the sack. All that I had succeeded in doing was to go out of circulation long enough for most of my movie connections to forget about me.

Life was a funny thing that happened to me on the way to the grave. I had never thought of my progress–perhaps we had better say my movement–through time as a triumphal march, but at this point I felt that I had stumbled. It is only when looking at an aerial shot taken by memory that I see how little was lost by my failure in the movie industry. If I have any talent at all, it is not for doing but for being. In the humblest way, this I was now given the opportunity to demonstrate.

I became a model.

THE DECLINING NUDE

This is an excerpt from a piece which Mr. Crisp wrote describing his experiences as an artist's model, published in 1949 in Little Reviews Anthology *(London: Methuen & Co.). It is the earliest writing of Mr. Crisp's I have been able to find.*–Ed.

One lunchtime, when I was lying stark naked on the throne of Hammersmith School of Art, a strange, fawnlike creature came and breathed down the back of my neck.

"Are you a model?" said he to me.

"What d'yer think?" said I to him.

Then he told me that some of the younger members of the

profession had decided that there ought to be a Models' Union. They were going to hold a meeting—he almost said "an underground meeting"—about this.

"What for?" I asked.

"Chiefly to raise the wages of models," the fawn replied.

"What for?" I asked again, and he disappeared—presumably back into one of Mr. Odets's plays. The union has now, however, been formed and wages raised. Being a model is a job that requires no references, no training, no previous experience, no specific ability—not even a thought in your head—and yet you can now earn 4s. an hour, 30s. a day, £7 10s. a week. What more can you ask?

A German sculptor once told me that in Italy models start their careers at 15 and graduate to the college in Rome. At the age of 25 they are considered superannuated, whereupon most of them marry and marry well.

In France and Germany a model has a social status somewhere between those of an actress and a prostitute. In England a model is merely a typist who was lonely, a dancer who was inadequate, or a down-and-out who was bored. "Doubtless," said the sculptor, "their characters are above reproach."

Like most actors, a model starts his career in the suburbs or even in the provinces and gradually wins his way to the heart of London. I began by doing a term at Derby. I took sticks of salt and strings of glass beads with which to do barter with the natives in hope that in exchange they would show me a narrow path between the overhanging factories to the art school. Everyone said that I would never live through this excursion to Derby, but Derby it was that died.

After the provinces, the suburbs: Willesden, Wimbledon,

Walthamstow. In a sense these schools offer the best "sittings" a model can hope to secure because the buildings are so well-heated and so well-arranged (with a lavatory in the models' dressing room). The school at Walthamstow is like a modern dream. Built in open, almost wild, country, it rises pillar after pillar, portico over portico, into the sky, and before it is a tremendous sweep of wide stone steps ending in a bed of nettles.

With the London schools, the rule is that the more venerable the establishment is, the more ill-equipped, dim, and dusty. The dirt, however, is compensated for by accessibility and a certain atmosphere of sophistication.

But at all schools, wherever they are situated, the ritual is much the same. Arriving about ten minutes before the class is due to start, the model calls at the office to sign in a book his name and, in very big schools, the name of the master for whom he is about to work. Then he climbs to the top of the building to the "Life" room, a large room with a wooden floor and a few "donkeys" and easels strewn about and, perhaps, even a few students. The atmosphere is like that of the reptile house at the Zoo. It smells of hot metal. In a dim corner of the room about two square feet are screened or curtained off. Here the model strips. Male models strip fully only in German schools. In England—and even in Paris—models wear a loincloth. By the time a model emerges the art master may have arrived to set the pose. The model steps onto the "throne," which is a small rostrum something like 18 inches high, and receives instructions which vary from an almost inaudible and totally indifferent phrase to the most elaborate description of the position required. On one of the first days of my life as a model I remember that an art master said wearily: "Take it easy. All you've got to do is sit." On the other hand, one of the famous art masters at St. Martin's School asked me to lie with chest facing downward and hips lying on their side. I put my elbows on the throne and threw my abdomen into the air like a dying salmon but it did not land on its side, so then I lay on my side and threw my thorax around. It did not fall prone. Standing over me with arms folded, the master said: "So you can't do it." At moments like this I try to think of that woman who posed as Ophelia for Mr. Millais. She lay for hours at a time clothed in a bath full of water, and when the apparatus for keeping the water warm failed, she refrained from disturbing the master by mentioning the fact. She died of pneumonia. I admire her more than I can say, for even poses that are not partially submerged are, after about the first 20 minutes, excruciating.

When a bomb was dropped on Goldsmiths' College and all the windows of the Life room fell in, I remained motionless. When the students had risen from the floor and dusted themselves, they congratulated me on my stoicism—my adherence to the Casablanca tradition. But of course the fact is that after remaining in one position for an hour, it is impossible to move at all. At such times as these the art master undoes the model like a deck chair, and as with a deck chair, he is always liable to get you inside out. Speaking of yoga, a model once said to me: "But once they've kept their arms over their heads for a while it is easier to leave them there than to bring them down. I think yoga is just a life of self-indulgence."

After the agony of relaxation for ten minutes or a quarter of an hour, the agony of getting back into pose again for 50 minutes or three quarters of an hour. And so on through alternate forms of suffering for seven hours a day for five days a week for 50 years, perhaps.

But all the same, posing has a very definite lure. For one thing, it is scandalous without being dangerous; for another, it is something you do with your body. The attraction of physical labor does not require Mr. Lawrence to publicize it.

Once there was a Polish model of a beauty like the sun, and on the second day of a continuous painting sitting at the Royal Academy School one of the students said to her, "But last week, Miss J., you had your left foot just a little bit further back." Without moving a muscle, Miss J. looked down from the throne and said, "I know I did. And what a damned fool I was."

But there is a penalty for such an attitude as this. To female models, posing is boring. When, in order to be paid, I rushed to the cashier's desk in St. Martin's School, I found two girls before me. While I waited behind them, the older said to the younger, "Well, d'you like posing?"

"Does anybody?" said the younger to the older.

"It's a way of filling time," was the reply, and I couldn't help adding: "between now and the grave."

When some years ago a model at last achieved by committing suicide that fame she had failed to win by posing, a journalist, who had herself once been a model, wrote an article entitled "Too Much Time to Think."

In a gallant effort to counteract boredom, the artist or art master always praises the model on the same principle as that which urges you to praise your charwoman. "No one can get the sink as clean as you can, Mrs. Phipps." For male models praise is not considered necessary. They are stimulated by posing and they, presumably, do not wait so eagerly either for the altar or for the grave. True, the professor at one of the universities sighs in automatic ecstasy before absolutely every model, but then, if you cut the heart out of a dogfish and fling it on the deck, it beats for eight hours. As a rule, a male model receives from masters a few words of hearty commiseration, but even these are perfunctory. At Toynbee Hall there is a four-hour sitting from 6 till 10 in the evening, at the beginning of which a model was once asked if he could not stand with arms outstretched "in a kind of crucifixion pose."

"Willingly," the man replied, "but I died after only three hours the last time, you remember."

It comes to this. You can either take easy poses and die of boredom or take difficult poses and die of an enlarged heart. "To each is given what defeat he will."

PART NINE

MR. CRISP, LIVE

Q: How has the price and quality of henna changed since you bought two pounds in World War II?

A: I've no idea, because by the time I was 40, somebody said you're dyeing your hair in order to seem younger, and though I wasn't, I said it was a reasonable criticism. So I had to think of a way of dyeing my hair so that you could see it was dyed, but so that you knew I was not trying to seem younger. So I gave up dyeing my hair red and dyed it this color. Blue.

I've no idea what's happened to henna since then.

Q: How do you think John Hurt did in portraying you in *The Naked Civil Servant* film?

A: Well, I was absolutely stunned by the trouble that he–everybody–connected with that production took. Very kindly, so that I could earn money for "technical advice," I was allowed on the location on about four different days. Of course, I never gave any advice. They kept saying, "Is it like it was?" And I said, "I want what Thames Television wants," because it didn't seem to me it mattered. But they were determined to get it right. They were determined to make Mr. Hurt over from head to foot. He allowed his eyebrows to be plucked from underneath to increase the distance between eyebrow and the eye. He wore five wigs in all, in order to pass from innocence (mouse color), through sin (two shades of scarlet), to two shades of this color. But first of all, I ought to say that no credit is due to me for the excellence of that program. The praise must go to Mr. Mackie, who wrote it, to Mr. Gold, who directed it, and to Mr. Hurt, who became my representative on earth.

Q: What have you been doing since you've been in this city and what do you do with leisure time at home in New York?

A: While I've been here I've either been photographed, or interviewed, or on the stage, or getting ready to go on the stage. I do a lot of sleeping, so I have to spend a lot of time in the room which my sponsors have found for me—just resting or sleeping. When you grow older, you need less sleep but more rest. You can't plan up sleep. When you're young you can say, Good heavens, I shan't get to bed till midnight tomorrow, so you go to bed and you sleep like mad. You can't do that when you get older. You wake up at 6 or 7 in the morning, whatever time you went to bed the night before. So you do need a lot of time for lying down.

As for my leisure time in New York, I do a lot of nothing. People become very restive when I tell them this. They say, "You don't do *nothing,* do you?" And I say, "I breathe and I blink." I don't know why this worries people. They hand you a lot of alternatives to save your soul: "You read a lot of books, surely," and I say I never do. "Well, you listen to the radio," and I don't have a radio. They keep this up. I don't know why they find it just unbearable that you go home and you don't do anything.

Q: Can you recommend any places to visit in New York?

A: I can't really. Although I've been, by invitation, to various places in New York, I wouldn't really recommend them. I should explain. New York is full of vast places in which you find yourself—twice the size of this entire auditorium—and all these places are exactly alike. Their walls are black, the floor is wood, the noise is deafening. It's like being on a doomed liner. You can hear the engines chugging, the lights flash, but no help comes. They're sort of teenage *Titanics.*

Q: Do I look 24 years old?

A: You *all* look 24 years old. If you don't look 24 years old, there's only one word of advice I can give you. Put it on with a brush.

Q: Do you believe in God?

A: Well, now, the last time You-Know-Who was mentioned, I began by saying I wouldn't like to say anything that gave offense. And someone in the audience said, "Why stop now?" But this is still something that worries me, so if at any moment anyone finds anything I say offensive, they have only to jump up and down, make a scene, and we will stop.

I believe, like most people, not that of which logic can convince me but what my nature inclines me to believe. This is so of nearly everybody. I am unable to believe in a God susceptible to prayer as petition. It does not seem to me to be sufficiently humble to imagine that whatever force keeps the planets turning in the heavens is going to stop what it's doing to give me a bicycle with three speeds.

But if God is the universe that encloses the universe, or if God is the cell within the cell, or if God is the cause behind the cause, then this I accept absolutely. And if prayer is a way of aligning your body with the forces that flow through the universe, then prayer I accept. But there is a worrying aspect about the idea of God. Like witchcraft or the science of the zodiac or any of these other things, the burden is placed *elsewhere*. This is what I don't like. You see, to me, *you* are the heroes of this hour. I do not think the earth was ever meant to be your home. I do not see the sky as a canopy held over your head by cherubs or see the earth as a carpet laid at your feet. You used to live an easy, lying-down life in the sea. But your curiosity and your courage prompted you to lift your head out of the sea and gasp this fierce element in which we live. They are sitting on Mars, with their little green arms folded, saying, "We can be reasonably certain there is no life on Earth because there the atmosphere is oxygen, which is so harsh that it corrupts metal." But you learned to *breathe* it. Furthermore, you crawled out of the sea, and you walked up and down the beach for centuries until your thighbones were thick enough to walk on land. It was a mistake, but you did it.

Once you have this view of your past—not that it was handed to you but that you did it—then your view of the future will
change. This terror you have of the atom bomb will pass.
Something will arise which will breathe radiation if *you*
learned to breathe oxygen.

So you don't have to worry. Don't keep looking into the sky
to see what is happening. Embrace the future. All you have to
do about the future is what you did about the past. Rely on
your curiosity and your courage, and ride through the night.

Q: How long has it taken you to get to where you are now,
and how much further do you want to go?

A: Well, it's taken all my life to get to where I am. My entire life has been a matter of chance. I never decided to do
anything. Everything has been given to me by others. I've
been handed forward in a fire basket from one person to another and finally got to America. I think that's really the best
way to tackle it. If you make decisions that you will do something, you'll be to blame. But if it's all done for you, you don't
have that problem. You can say, "They drove me to it."

How much further do I want to go? I don't think there really *is* anything else. I once lived in England, and now I live
in America. Where else could I go? And indeed, I not only live
in America, I live in New York. Now, I did live for a while in
Los Angeles, which is another earthly paradise. Everybody is
beautiful and everybody is rich. All the women are actresses
and all the men are lawyers and awards grow on trees. But of
course they know they're only playing. If you want to rule the
world, you have to live in New York. And I'm amazed to find

that without having done anything of my own accord, I have finally arrived in New York. And I'm very grateful to life that this has happened.

Q: Have you ever met the "great dark man"?

A: This question arises from the television program of my life. When I was told by Mr. Mackie that if he couldn't get all the jokes into the dialogue he would put them onto captions, I was absolutely astounded. I said, the screen will go black and the words will appear: "There is no great dark man"? He said yes. When I saw the movie, I accepted it. And no, I never found the great dark man because there *is* no great dark man. You are alone. It's always the same—it's never "out there," it's always in here. I once knew a woman with whom I discussed the theory of the great dark man and she said, "I've lived with a number of men and each one of them has had to be carried every step of the way."

Q: I understand you share a birthday with an equally famous personage. Do you think this is mere coincidence?

A: I was born on Christmas Day. Yes, I think we have to regard it as mere coincidence. I like being born on Christmas Day, although when I was a child I found Christmas embarrassing, terribly embarrassing. I'm glad to have reached the age where no one makes a fuss in my presence. When I was young my father gave me two shillings with which to buy a present for my mother. My mother gave me two shillings to buy a present for my father, and they both thanked me. It was terrible. I'm glad that nowadays, concerning Christmas, I can go on as though nothing unpleasant was happening.

Q: Do you ever baby-sit?

A: Well, I *have* baby-sat. Once many years ago I happened to see Merlin Peet, a friend of mine and a famous illustrator, and his wife, and they said they couldn't go out because the children had to be left and I said, I will sit with them; go out for a couple of hours and come back. Many years later, in an art gallery, I met Mrs. Peet with one of these children and she asked me, "Do you remember him? You once baby-sat with him. You don't seem to have done him any harm."

Q: Why did you move to New York?

A: I came to New York first in 1977, just for two and a half days, at the invitation of Mr. Bennett. I could never have come before because I could never have paid my fare. I had never earned more than 12 pounds a week my entire life–$25. It would have taken me two years to save up the money to come here. So I waited, and the day did come when Mr. Bennett– do you understand Mr. Bennett? He's the darling of the Shubert Theatre because he invented a show called *A Chorus Line*–and he invited me to come, and I came, and the moment I saw New York I wanted it. As my agent said, in a tired voice, "As this is the only preference you've ever expressed, we should do something about it." So we set about my becoming a resident alien. It took more than a year, and more than a thousand pounds, but now I am actually a resident alien. I've been a resident alien for two years. In another three years, if I learn the names of the Presidents, recite the Oath of Allegiance, and explain the Constitution, I can become a full-time American, and then I can commit my first murder.

But the reason I wanted to live here is that I realized that the difference between America and all other countries was that here everybody is your friend. This is the most astounding thing, if you come from any other country to America. When you get on a bus, for instance, you've hardly sat down before someone has said, "Where are you going?" and when you tell them, someone else says, "*This* bus doesn't go there." Within two minutes you've got the entire bus interested in your destination.

I live on the Lower East Side and am told that I am in perpetual danger. Now, I won't tempt Providence by saying I'm not; I will say that everyone in America who isn't hitting you over the head is your lifelong friend.

Q: Are you musically talented?

A: No, I am not musically talented, I'm happy to say. Music is another mistake. I should say more. Everything that has gone wrong with the world since the place was opened is due to music. Music is an insistent beat slightly more rapid than the heart, and it is accompanied by a few phrases repeated over and over and over till the entire tribe notices. Its purpose is to unite and arouse the male population, in years past usually for a waltz. Now you have no waltz, so you have a united and aroused population with nothing to do.

Q: When does self-pity end and pretension begin?

A: Oh, there is a point, but only you will know it. The difficulty is that once you start to cultivate your image, you do in a sense start to cultivate your exhibitionism. And exhibitionism is like a drug. You take a dose of it after a while that would kill anyone just starting out. So the day does have to come when you say, "Am I doing this to please myself, or am I doing it to annoy the neighbors?" You see, the desire to annoy the neighbors is just as ridiculous as the desire to placate the neighbors. What you have to ask yourself is this: If there were no praise, and no blame, who would I be then? *Then* you know who you are, and what your style is.

Q: Can boredom be elevated to an art?

A: No, indeed, it can't. Boredom is inexcusable, and worse is to say that other people are boring. When we say of somebody else that he is boring, it is ourselves we criticize because we have not made ourselves into that wide-open vessel into which people can pour their entire lives. Nothing is boring except a lie. Anyone who would tell the truth about himself is interesting. If people are not telling you the truth it's because they are afraid of you: you've said something to them which makes them guarded. This is of course the whole purpose of having an image, because it removes all those guarded assertions, all those generalities, all those platitudes. They are removed once a person knows from looking at you what he can profitably tell or ask of you.

Nobody ever talks to me about the weather.

Q: Do you still feel books are for writing, not for reading?

A: Yes, books are for writing. Do not read any more books. Everybody can write one little book, and it should be about himself. But if you read books, you will try to write literature, and that is always a mistake. It always makes your work like other people's work; it means we lose the sound of your voice. This is why books are a mistake. But they *are* a way of reaching the world, so you are allowed to write one as long as it is about yourself.

Q: Do you disapprove of people who watch television?

A: No, I like television, though I don't have time to watch a great deal.

In England, of course, the best television is American—without any doubt. If they're running fast and shooting straight, it's American. In England we have nobody of the magnitude of the great television stars of America. We have no one like Mr. Savalas or Raymond Burr. Raymond Burr is now the same *shape* as the screen—deliberately, I think, so that nothing else shall be needed.

Q: How do you cope with matters financial? Don't you hate modern banking?

A: I don't think I really know much about modern banking. But there is a great difference between the banks in America and the banks in England. In England banking really does look practically like a cottage industry. In King's

Road, Chelsea, there is a bank that appears to be about the size of this stage, and if I went in and said to one of the girls, "Is he in?" she would say, "I'll see." And if he was, she'd say, "Come on in," and I'd go and speak to him–the manager. In American banks you *never* meet the manager.

My money, such as it is, is in a bank on Madison Avenue, and the bank is the size of this theater. It is populated by elegant black ladies whose ankles are no thicker than other people's wrists. And the treatment you receive is wonderfully gracious. But of course when they see me they start to laugh because, you see, my money was in that bank for at least two years before I said, "I seem to have *two* accounts in your bank." The lady said yes. "Why do I have two accounts?" And she said, "I think you need an accountant." I've been given an accountant, and he is like a hamster. He sits in a little room in a nest of paper. I've never actually seen him put income tax returns into his teeth, but I think that's what he does. When I first went to see him, I took a small piece of paper and said, "This is a list of my resources and my income," and he said, "You're better organized than I am." So I don't expect very much from modern banking.

Q: What is the quickest remedy for a broken heart?

A: The quickest remedy is that you must learn not to value love because it is requited. It makes no difference whether your love is returned. Your love is of value to you because you give it. It's as though you gave me a present merely because you thought I would give you one in return. This won't do. If you have love to give, you give it, and you give it where it is needed, but never, never ask for anything in return. Once you've got that in your head, the idea of your heart being broken will disappear.

Q: How have you managed to make the transition from middle age to senior citizen?

A: Oh, that's been easy. It's the beginning of middle age that is difficult. There does come a time when you know—and if you know, everyone else knows—that you are 40. You don't feel much different, and you have to school yourself to behave as though you were 40. But later on when you are in fact old, you are aware all the time that you are old, and this is a great help because it means you do behave a bit better.

But of course I have not learned to behave any better. There is a story told that Somerset Maugham once began a public speech with the words, "There are advantages in growing old," and then he paused so long that the audience rose to go to his aid. "I was just trying to think of one," he said finally. It's not for me to go on where Mr. Maugham left off, but I do, and I will tell you the advantage of growing old. As it's toward the end of the run, you can overact appallingly.

Q: What is your definition of a movie star?

A: To me, a movie star has to be something you couldn't have invented for yourself if you'd sat up all night.

Q: What makes you happy?

A: I think my only pastime is people. I have no hobbies, I have no recreations, as I've explained, I never read books; when I'm not out in the world I'm at home recharging my batteries. I go home and I rest–totally. But when I'm out of doors I'm with the world. What makes me happy is the feeling that I have at last, after all these years, entered into the world, from which I was exiled for so long.

Q: To whom did Tallulah Bankhead say what in *Fallen Angel?*

A: One of the mysteries to me about Mr. Coward's plays which are still shown, one of which is *Fallen Angel,* is when you see them now how totally empty they are. But when I saw them originally I can remember being absolutely delighted with every line. Looking back, I can't see even where the jokes were. There's a moment in the second act of *Fallen Angel*–the play is about two women who agree that however badly they behave they will be friends afterward–when the Frenchman with whom they've both had an affair arrives in London, and they're both free to make a dash for him to do whatever they like. They will be friends later. They stage a dinner for him which takes up the entire second act, but he never arrives. And they get more and more intoxicated, and there's a moment–which the audience found hilarious– when Edna Best says, "I've had much too much too much to eat already," and Tallulah Bankhead says, "So have I, but we must go on." I think his greatness was, he wrote the lines actresses longed to say. That's the key to Mr. Coward.

Q: How would you feel if suddenly the world turned against you?

A: I would be puzzled now because the world has turned toward me. That doesn't mean I couldn't meet people who were discreetly embarrassed that I was there, who would obviously be standing around later saying, "I'm grateful he's gone." That wouldn't surprise me because I'm so used to that from the past. If suddenly the press started to savage me, make fun of me, then I would worry. There was once in England an actress called Margaret Lockwood, and she was an extremely cultured movie actress by British standards. The moment she started to be a success—it's true it was in melodramas like *The Wicked Lady* and *The Man in Grey*—the press turned on her. I thought she must be absolutely *dazed*. She was only doing her job, and the press didn't say, "This really wasn't a part that suited her"; they made fun of her in every possible way.

Q: But not because she'd been doing anything very different than she'd done before...

A: She never did anything she hadn't done before except that she was now playing the leading lady.

Now if that happened to me, it would happen on a smaller scale because I don't make movies which millions of people see. But if the press totally turned against me I would think: Well, I'm doing what I've done before, it's old hat, the world has passed on, and I'm doing it wrong. I would of course first of all examine myself. The first thing you do is to decide how much of the response you deserve. You'll never get on with anything if you start immediately with saying, "They're absolutely unjust, they're absolutely unfair–they say that because they're jealous." All this is a complete waste of time. The first thing to say is, "How much of this is true, and of what is true, how much can I alter?"

What the world sees in you is their truth. It's not *the* truth. But always examine yourself first as a cause for what's gone wrong.

Q: Without guilt?

A: Without guilt, but also without false innocence.

I suppose we should now stop, but before we do I would like first of all to thank you for staying so *long,* and then to say that of course I know that there are people who don't give a fig for the big time, who don't want a public image–but I'm trying to speak to anybody here who may feel that the band always seems to be playing in another street. And when I say, "The door is not locked, go to where the band is playing," I don't want anyone to say, "But I haven't a thing to wear!" All you have to wear are your wonderful, wonderful selves. And what I think gives me the right to say so is this: If I, who am nothing, who am nobody, have got from London to Australia to Canada and finally to America, then anyone can do it. And what makes the message urgent is that the benefits are very considerable, although they may not be what you imagine. People rush up to me in the street and they say, "Now that you're rich and famous..." They never get any further, because I stop them. As you all know perfectly well, I am not famous, I am notorious. And if I am rich, it is because I have taken my wages in people.

You are my reward—and thank you.